The Voter's Guide to Healthcare:
A Non-partisan, Candid, and Relevant Look
at Politics and Healthcare in America

By Den Bishop

First published by Dog Ear Publishing
8888 Keystone Crossing
Suite 1300
Indianapolis, IN 46240
www.dogearpublishing.net

ISBN: 978-145757-071-1

This book is printed on acid-free paper.
Printed in the United States of America

Contents

Preface

WE ARE APPROXIMATELY A DECADE removed from the signing of the Affordable Care Act (ACA). Progressives promised that the law would fix healthcare problems in America. Conservatives warned that the law would ruin healthcare in America. The political divide over healthcare has not healed, as healthcare is once again taking its place on the throne as the king of political issues.

You are probably familiar with the problems. Healthcare is expensive. Healthcare and health insurance are complicated. In spite of the high cost of healthcare, our health outcomes are not comparably favorable to those of nations with lower costs. Moreover, approximately more than twenty-seven million people in America have no health insurance. We have cost, complexity, quality, and coverage problems. It is not difficult to see why voters have named healthcare as the number-one election topic in the 2020 presidential election.

I am not a physician. I don't know how to heal anyone's personal medical condition. I am a healthcare consultant whose primary business sits at the intersection of employers, insurance companies, healthcare providers, and the government. I see how these stakeholders come together like a traffic cop sees cars and buses in Times Square. The healthcare stakeholders are honking, and they all want priority in the intersection. Sitting on the curb on the side of the road and criticizing the drivers seems easier . . . and safer; however, I feel compelled to grab my whistle to try to bring order to the chaos in the intersection. If you could see what I see, you would grab your whistle and get in the middle of the traffic too.

This book's purpose is to not only educate but also help inoculate the reader against the healthcare debate's highly contagious communicable diseases. Let's call the condition Healthcare Reform Fever (HRF). Symptoms of HRF include the following:

- **Uncontrollable Anger**—The mention of healthcare reform, health insurance companies, Obamacare, or repeal and replace causes your blood pressure and voice to rise.

- **Partisanship**—The source of what you hear is more important than the content. You agree or disagree based on who says it rather than what is being said. Your voter registration card does not automatically disengage your brain and your heart.

- **Finger Pointing**—Your index finger is in a permanent extended position, looking for someone to blame.

- **Status Quo Protection**—You are trying to protect the things that are good for you but aren't willing to give on some things, maybe even some big things, to solve the problem for all.

- **Victimhood**—Politicians have convinced you that you can't have what you deserve because of what someone else has or does. (Here's a secret . . . it isn't all the insurance companies' fault.)

- **Gullibility**—You fall for the half-truths and fake news of campaign promises. You actually thought you could keep your plan if you liked it and that the ACA was not only going to be repealed but also replaced.

If you are experiencing any of these symptoms, you should consume this book slowly and on a full stomach. If symptoms are severe or have lasted more than four hours, please consult a physician. Do not operate heavy machinery immediately after reading this book. However, if you are symptom-free and want to make sure you personally avoid these nasty symptoms, then this book is for you (with no restrictions)!

In an attempt to prevent the onset and spread of HRF, *The Voter's Guide to Healthcare* looks at America's healthcare financing system as a patient. We cannot prescribe a treatment for the patient without first understanding the patient's problems and accurately diagnosing the underlying conditions causing the problems. To prescribe a solution without first examining and diagnosing the patient would be political malpractice!

- **Section 1 – Getting to Know the Patient**—The first section of the book familiarizes you with the patient. Think of it like that lengthy health history you fill out the first time you visit a physician's office to give the physician the background necessary prior to diagnosis.

- **Section 2 - Diagnosing Symptoms**—The second section analyzes the symptoms causing problems in our current healthcare system. The symptoms include intense pain in the pocketbook, confusion, and general disability. The severity of the symptoms requires some diagnostic analysis.

- **Section 3 - Treatment Options**—After you understand the patient and its symptoms, the book explores various treatment options currently being suggested by our politicians.

- **Section 4 - Recommended Course of Treatment**—The final segment of the book is about the treatment plan I recommend to permanently restore the patient's health.

The greatest good of health insurance is to proactively connect the at-risk patients with the medical providers and programs that give them the best chance of getting better. Unfortunately, our current misaligned healthcare system often creates hurdles, rather than connections, for patients and providers. The result is an expensive, frustrating, and poorly performing healthcare system. By intentionally connecting and aligning the public and private financing sources of our healthcare system, we can free up the healthcare heroes to get to the important work of relieving pain, curing disease, and saving lives. That's the healthcare reform we really need!

Introduction:

Healthcare Is #1?

Why is healthcare the number-one issue among voters? Here are a few numbers to provide insight to that question.

#1

Healthcare is the number-one expenditure for the federal government.

Healthcare is the fastest growing expense for the federal government.

Healthcare is the number-one reason people file for personal bankruptcy.

Healthcare is the number-one job-creating industry.

Healthcare has become the largest employment industry in America.

$28,386

The total average cost for health insurance for a family of four receiving employer-sponsored health insurance in 2019 is $28,386. This includes the amount paid by the employer, the employee payroll deductions for premiums, and the average family's out-of-pocket cost for medical services.

27,462,000

Approximately 27 million people in the US have no health insurance protection.

58%

People in the US die at a 58% higher rate than people in other economically developed countries from conditions that could have been diagnosed and effectively treated by care that is available within the US healthcare system.

We have a healthcare system that has cost problems, does not cover everyone, and leaves Americans dying unnecessarily. Considering these facts, it is no wonder that politicians are tossing healthcare solutions around like political footballs. Can't the government just give us all free healthcare? Can't we just get the government out of healthcare? Is the government the solution, or is the government to blame? None of these questions has a clear answer, but one thing *is* clear: Opinions on the government's role in healthcare are kind of like belly buttons . . . everybody has one!

Red, Blue, and Purple

The Voter's Guide to Healthcare is not intended to sway readers to either the left or the right politically. If you side with MSNBC today, you will still lean left after reading this. Likewise, if you can't get enough Fox News, this will do nothing to quench your Conservative thirst. The healthcare issue is neither blue nor red. It is purple! Purple is what is created when you perfectly blend blue and red. Healthcare is an all-in combination of blue and red because it impacts each and every one of us without regard to race, religion, income, gender, or politics.

Healthcare is inextricably political because it is about people and money. However, *political* does not have to mean *partisan*. A partisan viewpoint is naturally prejudiced for or against something. Think of it like discussions of race: A sensitive issue can be racial and still be discussed with dignity, respect, and honesty. *Racial* means it has to do with race but is not biased. However, an issue or viewpoint that becomes *racist* crosses the line of prejudice. In the same vein, an issue can also be *political* and discussed with dignity, respect, and honesty. However, an issue or viewpoint that becomes *partisan* crosses the line of prejudice. To adequately address the massive healthcare challenge, we must be willing to set aside our individual partisan prejudice to discuss this important political issue without undue bias. This book explores the programs through which health insurance is delivered today, as well as the problems we face, the proposals being debated, and a plan forward to heal the healthcare system.

I view healthcare as one of our most challenging social-justice issues, and far and away the greatest economic challenge facing our country. We have an economic imbalance because our current tax structure can't adequately cover existing expenditures, and we have a social imbalance with more than twenty-seven million people who have no health insurance protection. My goal is to simplify and educate so that you won't be swayed, moved, or manipulated by fake news or truth-twisting campaign promises. Knowledge is power. Let's get health strong!

SECTION 1:

GETTING TO KNOW THE PATIENT: THE PEOPLE AND PROGRAMS

WHAT HAPPENS WHEN YOU ARRIVE for an appointment with a new physician? You get the clipboard! The next half hour of your life is spent putting ballpoint pen to paper to describe your health history, your family's medical history, and your exercise, diet, stress, and social habits. Why does the office need all this information? Because treating you without first understanding you, your history, and your family's history would be considered malpractice. The physician must understand where you came from, how you got here, and who you are.

People in the US receive their health insurance through a variety of public and private insurance programs. A basic understanding of these programs is similar to the personal and family health history forms in an initial physician office visit. Talking about how to reform healthcare without first understanding the programs through which it is delivered today and the challenges that these programs, and the participants in them, face is like having surgery prior to diagnosing the problem. We must understand where we are today, how we got here, and how other programs impact our nation's healthcare DNA. The baseline understanding sets the stage for further examination and treatment recommendations.

1

HEALTH INSURANCE COVERAGE OF THE TOTAL POPULATION, 2017

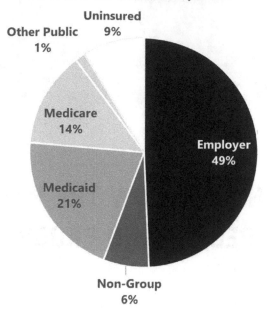

Source: Kaiser Family Foundation. "Health Insurance Coverage of the Total Population." Kff.org. 2019.

Should we expand Medicare eligibility? Should we just move to Medicare for all? Why did some states expand Medicaid eligibility while others have not? Should a public-plan option be added to Obamacare? Should the tax expenditure for employer-sponsored health insurance be capped? Why are prescription drugs so much more expensive in the US than in other countries? Why do we have so many uninsured Americans? These questions, and others, cannot be answered appropriately without an understanding of the programs and people in them.

This section of the Voter's Guide introduces you to your family members in the American healthcare system.

Chapter 1:

Medicare Basics

What Is Medicare?

MEDICARE IS A FEDERAL HEALTH insurance program that covers people age sixty-five or older, along with certain younger individuals who are disabled or have end-stage renal disease. As of May 2019, Medicare covered 60,963,217 individuals.

Traditional Medicare

Medicare is not one complete health insurance program; it is a series of health insurance component options. (1)

- Medicare Part A covers inpatient services and typically does not require a premium. It includes a $1,364 deductible and has limits on the number of inpatient days covered per benefit period.

- Medicare Part B covers outpatient, physician, and professional services. Part B requires monthly participant premiums. The standard premium is $135.50 per month. The premiums increase based on income above $85,000 per year and can rise to $460.50 per month. Medicare Part B includes a $185 annual deductible and 20% coinsurance for most services.

- Medicare Part D covers prescription drugs. Prescription drug plans are administered and sold by private insurance companies. The average base premium for a Part D plan is $40 per month. Similar to Part B, additional premiums are required for individuals with income above $85,000 per year.

The combination of Medicare Parts A, B, and D creates a comprehensive medical plan. However, the plan participant is still subject to deductible and coinsurance out-of-pocket exposure. Medicare Supplement plans are available to cover out-of-pocket expenses and items not typically covered by Medicare.

Medicare Advantage

Medicare Part C is also known as Medicare Advantage (MA). MA plans are private insurance alternatives to traditional Medicare coverage. MA participants opt out of traditional Medicare and receive all their coverage through the private market. MA plans use provider networks similar to employer-sponsored coverage. Premiums and coverage provisions vary by plan; some plans have no deductible, and some plans are available for zero premium. Approximately 34% of all Medicare enrollees participate in MA plans. The number of participants doubled from eleven million in 2010 to twenty-two million in 2019. (2) The popularity of private alternatives to traditional Medicare is growing.

Approximately 80% of Medicare participants have some type of private insurance through either a Medicare Supplement or an MA plan. Medicare is considered a public insurance program, but it is delivered through a combination of public and private insurance providers. Voters could be confused when the terms "Medicare for all" and "single-payer" are used together, but today's Medicare is far from being a single-payer program. Medicare is a true public-private partnership.

MEDICARE ADVANTAGE ENROLLMENT

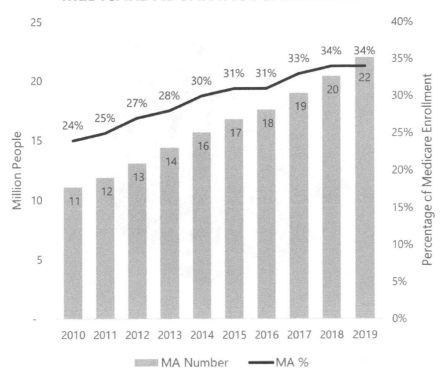

Source: Kaiser Family Foundation. "Medicare Advantage, Figure 1, Enrollment In Medicare Advantage has nearly doubled over the past decade." Kff.org. June 2019.

How Is Medicare Funded?

Medicare is funded annually through payroll taxes, premiums paid by participants, general federal government revenue transfers, and a list of smaller contributors, such as interest and taxes from benefits. It is important to note that premiums paid by Medicare beneficiaries cover less than 15% of the annual cost. (3) The program is funded primarily by sources other than participant premiums. Those who simply point to Medicare's premiums being lower than the premiums of private insurance may not understand that more than 85% of the premium is subsidized from other revenue sources. Would an expansion of Medicare eligibility also include an expansion of the government's heavy subsidy of the required premiums?

MEDICARE REVENUE SOURCES, 2017

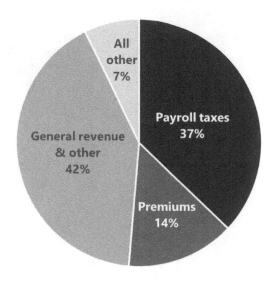

Source: Centers for Medicare and Medicaid Services. "2019 Annual Report of the Boards of Trustees of the Federal Hospital Insurance and Federal Supplementary Medical Insurance Trust Funds." Cms.gov. April 22, 2019.

Medicare's near-term solvency is in jeopardy, according to Medicare's trustees. The Medicare Hospital Insurance trust fund is projected to be depleted and to become insolvent in 2026. (4)

A Ponzi scheme is a fraudulent financial program in which money coming in from new investors is paid out to prior investors. Early enrollees are fine, but late arrivers get left empty-handed. The result is that no money or assets are left in the end. Although there is a trust fund, Medicare is a cash-flow business and must be constantly funded. In some ways, you could consider the Medicare trust funds and financing to be a type of benefit Ponzi scheme because Medicare taxes paid by you and your employer do not go into a fund to pay for your future Medicare benefits. Instead, the money you and your employer pay *this year* pay for Medicare beneficiaries *this year*. If the trust fund had to fund Medicare without additional revenue sources, the fund would be exhausted before the end of May in the first year.

The cash-flow Ponzi structure might seem bad enough, but there is a further financing complication. As of December 2018, the federal government has borrowed $304.3 billion from the Medicare trust funds through intragovernmental debt. This is almost the entire trust fund balance. (3)

So, what does this really mean? It means the money in the Medicare trust funds has been loaned to the federal government and has already been spent on other things. A comparison to your 401(k) might help explain. Assume you put $10,000 per year into your 401(k) for twenty years. After the twenty years, you have deposited $200,000 into your account, but you decided to take annual loans in the amount of $10,000 out at the end of each year, totaling $200,000 in loans. You did not repay any of the loans. If you retire at the end of the twenty-year period, how much money do you have in your 401(k) for retirement? The simple answer is *almost nothing*, because you borrowed everything you deposited to spend on other things. The federal government has done the exact same thing to the Medicare trust funds.

Medicare and American Demographics

Federal government net Medicare expenditures have been growing as a percentage of gross domestic product (GDP). The combination of changing demographics and healthcare inflation creates financial pressure for Medicare. Between 2000 and 2018, the number of workers in the country per beneficiary dropped from 4.0 to 3.0. Put another way, in 2000, four workers were paying taxes to fund Medicare for every one person receiving Medicare benefits. Now just three workers are paying Medicare taxes for each beneficiary. This ratio will continue its downward slide over the next decade as baby boomers continue to age into Medicare.

MEDICARE DEMOGRAPHIC PRESSURE

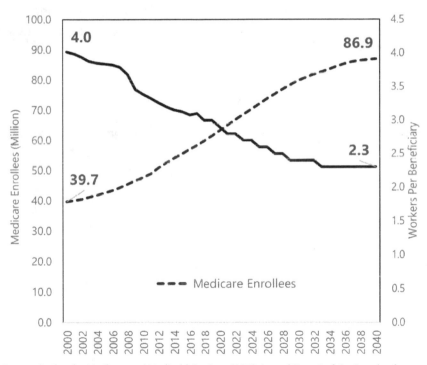

Source: Centers for Medicare and Medicaid Services. "2019 Annual Report of the Boards of Trustees of the Federal Hospital Insurance and Federal Supplementary Medical Insurance Trust Funds." Cms.gov. April 22, 2019.

The result of the demographic shift is intense financial pressure on Medicare's sustainability within the current tax structure. Does this mean Medicare will financially crash and go out of business? No, but it does mean that Medicare will need more money to pay its bills than the current financing structure creates. Some combination of reduced expenditures, increased premiums, and increased taxes will be needed. Status quo means acceleration of the federal deficit through a growing Medicare funding shortfall.

Medicare Recap

- Medicare is the public insurance program for older Americans.

- The program cost is heavily subsidized by payroll taxes and general tax revenues.

- Medicare is delivered through a public-private partnership.

- The combination of healthcare inflation and the demographic shift that creates fewer workers per Medicare beneficiary threatens Medicare's solvency.

What's Next?

The combination of the demographic aging in America and healthcare inflation puts tremendous pressure on the Medicare trust funds and on the federal budget in total. Medicare is not adequately financed under its current structure. Politicians on the left are lining up in support of Medicare eligibility expansion or even Medicare for all without discussing the details of how this eligibility expansion would either help or hinder the current Medicare financing challenge. The debate regarding who is, and who is not, eligible for Medicare is sure to be among America's most hotly debated subjects in the coming years.

Sources

(1)   Kaiser Family Foundation. "Medicare Advantage 2019 Spotlight: First Look." Kff.org. October 16, 2018.

(2)   Kaiser Family Foundation. "Medicare Advantage, Figure 1. Enrollment in Medicare Advantage has nearly doubled over the past decade." Kff.org. June 6, 2019.

(3)   Centers for Medicare and Medicaid Services. "2019 Annual Report of the Boards of Trustees of the Federal Hospital Insurance and Federal Supplementary Medical Insurance Trust Funds." Cms.gov. April 22, 2019.

(4)   Alan Rappeport. "Social Security and Medicare Funds Face Insolvency, Report Finds." *New York Times.* April 22, 2019.

Chapter 2:

Medicaid Basics

What Is Medicaid?

MEDICAID IS THE PUBLIC HEALTH insurance program for low-income Americans. Medicaid, combined with the Children's Health Insurance Program (CHIP), covers 72,918,167 individuals: 66,346,562 are covered by Medicaid and 6,571,605 by CHIP. The Medicaid and CHIP data book estimates that 29.1% of the population was enrolled in Medicaid or CHIP at some point in 2017. (1)

The program is a collaboration between the federal government and individual states, with each paying a share of the cost. The percentage of the cost paid by the federal government varies by state but averaged 61.5% in 2017. Montana had the highest percentage paid by the federal government, at 80%, and New York had the lowest, at 48.8%. (2)

Similar to Medicare, Medicaid utilizes a combination of public and private insurance programs. More than two-thirds of Medicaid enrollees are in a private managed-care program. (3) States choose whether to contract with private insurance companies or whether to use a public fee for a service benefit and provider payment system.

ACA and Medicaid

The ACA attempted to reduce the number of uninsured Americans by expanding Medicaid eligibility. Medicaid eligibility and benefits varied by state prior to the ACA, and the law mandated that states expand eligibility to a common standard and provide consistent benefit levels. The common income eligibility standard created within the ACA was effectively 133% of federal poverty level (FPL). For the first few years, the federal government paid 100% of the cost of newly eligible Medicaid individuals, with a schedule declining to 90% by 2020. The Supreme Court deemed the action by the federal government through the ACA to be unconstitutional coercion, determining that the federal government could not force the expense associated with Medicaid expansion on states. The remedy for the unconstitutionality was to give states the choice of whether or not to expand Medicaid eligibility to the federal standard.

The Supreme Court's remedy decision resulted in state choice regarding Medicaid eligibility expansion. As of this writing, fourteen states have chosen to not comply with the ACA expansion:

- Alabama
- Florida
- Georgia
- Kansas
- Mississippi
- Missouri
- North Carolina
- Oklahoma
- South Carolina
- South Dakota
- Tennessee
- Texas
- Wisconsin
- Wyoming

If the federal government is covering 90% of the ongoing cost for newly eligible individuals, why wouldn't a state expand eligibility? It could simply be revenge politics, with Republican governors resisting the Democrat-authored expansion. It could also be fear of a false promise. Although the ACA requires that the federal government will pay 90% of the cost for newly eligible individuals, there is no permanent guarantee from the federal government. In fact, the Congressional Budget Office (CBO) financially scored the concept of limiting the federal government's funding for Medicaid in November 2013—before the January 1, 2014, expansion even started. Whether Congress ever intends to reduce the federal government's commitment to funding Medicaid expansion is not known, but the CBO continues to provide financial estimates for shifting financial responsibility to states by capping the federal government's spending on Medicaid.

Medicaid Enrollment

The number of individuals covered by Medicaid and CHIP has grown significantly, even with some states electing to not expand eligibility. Enrollment has more than doubled since 2000.

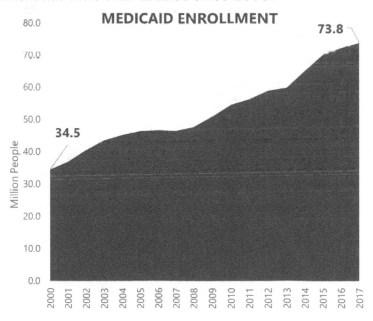

Source: MACStats. "Exhibit 10 - Medicaid Enrollment and Total Spending Levels and Annual Growth." Macpac.gov. December 2018.

Medicaid Assistance Gap

The ACA created a health insurance subsidy system for individuals in families earning between 100% and 400% of the FPL. The fourteen states that did not expand Medicaid eligibility in accordance with the ACA have varying eligibility requirements. Low-income adults earning less than 100% of the FPL and not qualifying for Medicaid assistance based on their state's eligibility fall into the Medicaid Assistance Gap. They don't make enough to qualify for an ACA subsidy, and Medicaid is not available to them in their state. For many voters, leaving the neediest in our society with no health insurance assistance is a difficult social-justice pill to swallow.

Medicaid Recap

- Medicaid is the public insurance program for lower-income Americans.
- The program is funded through a federal-state partnership.
- Medicaid expansion was the primary vehicle used to reduce the number of uninsured Americans through the ACA.
- The ACA expansion of Medicaid was deemed unconstitutional, which allowed states to choose to expand, or not.
- Non-expansion states have the social-justice challenge of providing no health insurance assistance to some of the neediest adults in society.

What's Next?

The fourteen states that have not expanded eligibility will continue to face pressure to do so. Leaving the economically neediest in society without health insurance coverage is a social-justice question and challenge that will not go away.

The federal government is already signaling that it may need to find ways to contain its Medicaid spending. The options for which the CBO has produced financial estimates provide an indication of potential future direction: putting significant financial pressure on states.

States will continue to find innovative ways to contain Medicaid pricing. Medicaid is delivered on a state-specific delivery platform. Each state effectively has its own network or provider-reimbursement strategy. Expect significant state pressure to control spending as inflation and enrollment continue to grow.

Sources

(1)   Medicaid and CHIP Payment and Access Commission. "MACStats: Medicaid and CHIP data book." Macpac.gov. December 2018.

(2)   Kaiser Family Foundation. "Federal and State Share of Medicaid Spending." Kff.org. 2019.

(3)   Robin Rudowitz, Rachel Garfield, and Elizabeth Hinton. "10 Things to Know about Medicaid: Setting the Facts Straight." Kaiser Family Foundation. Kff.org. March 6, 2019.

Chapter 3:

Employer-Sponsored Health Insurance

ON SEPTEMBER 24, 2013, POLITICAL enemies President Barack Obama and Senator Ted Cruz, who rarely agreed on any subject, made almost identical statements related to employer-sponsored health insurance. President Obama referred to employer-sponsored health insurance as a "historic accident," while Senator Cruz referred to it as a "historic anomaly." Both believed the employer role in healthcare was misplaced, with President Obama believing the government should play a bigger role in replacing the employer, and Senator Cruz believing the consumer should replace the employer's power in healthcare. Either way, both believed the employer-sponsored system was wrong and broken. So, how did employers get themselves into the health insurance business, and what is their appropriate role?

Employers entered the health-insurance arena as a response to the World War II (WWII) wage freezes. The government was worried about hyperinflation, and thus, instituted wage freezes to slow inflation. Employers looked for non-wage alternatives to attract and retain workers, and health insurance became a tax-preferred alternative to compete for labor. The WWII wage freeze obviously ended, but the tax-preferred incentive to obtain health insurance through your job has continued without interruption.

With approximately 159 million people under age sixty-five covered by employer-sponsored health insurance, more Americans get their health insurance coverage through employers than through any other method. (1) The total number of people covered by employer-sponsored health insurance has not changed significantly since the ACA was implemented, and the CBO forecasts that ten years from now, the number of Americans receiving health insurance through this system will remain at the same 159 million. This projection is in spite of a federal mandate requiring employers to offer health insurance coverage to full-time employees, cost increases that continue to outpace inflation, and the launch of a subsidized individual health-insurance exchange system that guarantees coverage with full preexisting-condition protection.

Participation and Mandates

The ACA created two different health insurance mandates. First, individuals are required to purchase health insurance coverage, and second, large employers must offer health insurance to their full-time employees. Employers with fewer than fifty full-time employees are not required to offer health insurance. The prevalence of offering health insurance shrinks dramatically as the number of employees shrinks. Targeting small employers with a mandate would have significantly increased the number of Americans receiving health insurance through their employers. The perception that this requirement would create an additional burden threatening small businesses outweighed the desire to reduce the number of uninsured Americans, resulting in the mandate's small-business exemption.

Large employers, defined as having fifty or more full-time employees, must offer their full-time employees affordable comprehensive health insurance coverage. Employers who do not offer coverage are subject to an annualized penalty of $2,320 per full-time employee.

If the plan is offered but does not meet ACA value and affordability requirements, the employer faces an annual penalty of $3,480 per full-time employee who receives a subsidy through the Marketplace.

The mandate did not create an increase in employer-sponsored insurance coverage. Targeting large employers with the mandate served as a barrier to keep large employers from abandoning their health insurance programs. Small employers, who are exempt from the mandate, have seen a decrease in health insurance offer rates.

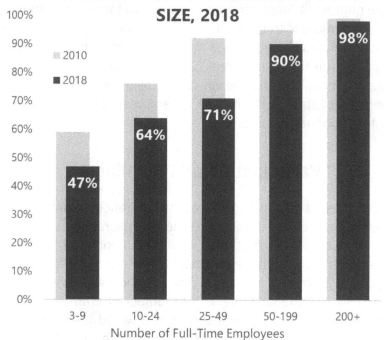

PERCENTAGE OF EMPLOYERS OFFERING HEALTH INSURANCE BY SIZE, 2018

Source: Kaiser Family Foundation. "Employer Health Benefits Annual Survey 2018, Figure 2.2, Percentage of Firms Offering Health Benefits, by Firm Size, 1999-2018." Kff.org. October 3, 2018.

Cost Increases

The average total employer-plus-employee cost for employer-sponsored health insurance for a family of four in 2019 was $28,386. (2) Let's put this number in perspective. For this amount, you could have paid for a full year of undergraduate pre-med tuition and fees at the University of Texas, bought a brand-new Honda Fit at full sticker price, blown $800 on a Tory Burch purse, and still had enough money to take a friend to dinner and margaritas at Chuy's in Austin to celebrate. Remember, this healthcare cost isn't a one-time expense; it is like paying for college and buying a new car *every year*!

Costs continue to rise faster than wages—and faster than the economy—for both employers and employees. Health insurance costs have risen at approximately four times the growth rate in household income, and a disproportionate share of the increasing cost is passed through to the employee. The combined per-paycheck and out-of-pocket expenses for employees have increased 109% between 2007 and 2017, according to the Milliman Medical Index. (3,4)

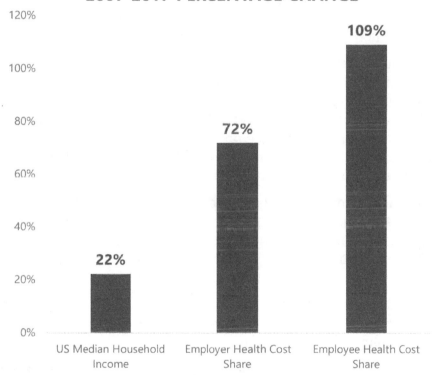

2007-2017 PERCENTAGE CHANGE

Sources: Christopher Girod, Susan Hart, and Scott Weltz. Figure 8. "2017 Milliman Medical Index." Milliman.com. May 16, 2017; Milliman, Inc. Figure 9. "2007 Milliman Medical Index." Milliman.com. May 1, 2007.

The ACA did little to lower the cost of health insurance for employers or their workers. In fact, a case could be made that the Medicare cost-shifting, coverage mandates, Obamacare Marketplace pricing disasters, and industry fees turned the employer-sponsored insurance market into the naïve tourist who became easy prey for professional healthcare pickpockets.

Reluctant Employer Responsibility

With more Americans receiving their health insurance through their employers than through any other source, employers play a vital role in funding and administering health insurance. Employers pay the majority of the cost and provide important enrollment, billing, and communication services. They take on these financial and administrative roles because health insurance is an important employee attraction-and-retention tool. For many, health insurance is more than an employee expectation; it is a required element of compensation.

Health insurance premium rates in employer coverage are based on the group of covered employees and family members. Rates per person are based on the plan selected, such as HMO vs PPO, and on family tier, such as employee-only or employee-plus-spouse. The rates are the same for every employee in the same plan and family tier. The rates for each employer are different and are determined with different methods based on the number of eligible employees.

- **Small Group (<50 full-time employees)**—The ACA regulates the rating methodology for groups with fewer than fifty employees. The rates are determined by the plan design, network, age mix, and geographic location of the covered individuals and are not based on health status or claims history.

- **Large Group (≥50 full-time employees)**—The cost of health insurance for large employers is heavily influenced by the claim costs of the group.

The majority of Americans who receive their health insurance through large employers are covered by some form of self-insurance. Department of Labor filings show that 83% of participants receive their health insurance through self-insured plans. (5) "Self-insured" means that your employer, and not Blue Cross, United, Cigna, Aetna, etc., is really the insurance company. The insurance company builds the network and administers the claims, but it is the employer's money that pays the claims and bears the risk. Lower claims mean lower business expense for the self-funded employer. Higher claims mean higher business expense. Think of the self-funded employer plan like an expense account: An employee or covered family member incurs an eligible medical expense, and the employer covers the expense, less the deductible and coinsurance.

"Fully insured" refers to health plans that pay fixed monthly premium rates to insurance companies based on monthly enrollment. The rates are determined annually. Health status, claims history, and known preexisting medical conditions are primary drivers of the required insurance rates. Whether self-funded or fully insured, the claims cost for the covered population ultimately determines the cost.

There are no preexisting medical condition protections for the employer rates. The individual who has a preexisting condition cannot be denied coverage or charged more, but the employer who covers that individual bears the financial burden whether the employer is self-funded or fully insured.

Community rating in health insurance means all participants pay the same premium for the same coverage without regard to individual health status or claims history. Employer-sponsored health insurance could be considered community-rated because all employees within a group pay the same rate, but it is important to note that your coworkers are your community for health insurance. If you work for a company with more than fifty employees, the cost of health insurance for your company and for you is determined by the health of your coworkers and their covered family members. Would an understanding of this reality cause people to look at their coworker community differently? Health insurance cost increases are not driven by insurance companies; they are created within your employee community.

Let's use car insurance to shed light on the health insurance reality. If car insurance were an employee benefit, the cost of car insurance for every employee inside the company would be the same. The car insurance would also be available to spouses and children. Bad drivers would be mixed with good drivers. Those who drove more-expensive cars, had much longer commutes, and had more frequent accidents would pay the same as those with less-expensive cars and no accidents. Drivers would enjoy preexisting automobile protection! Car insurance would also be administratively easier because the employer would deduct the cost from the paycheck, and the cost would be tax-deductible.

Let's assume the employer is self-funded for its employees' car insurance. More accidents mean greater expense for the employer. Let's assume the rate of inflation for car insurance is more than double the rate at which the employer can increase the prices for its products and services. To add to the equation, let's say the federal government has passed legislation requiring large employers to offer car insurance or pay a penalty to not offer such insurance. What action does this employer facing our theoretical car-insurance mandate take? Remember, the employer can't charge more to employees who have accidents or speeding tickets.

The likely actions of the employer would be to (1) shift car insurance premium increases to employees to manage the company expense and (2) increase deductibles so participants would pay more when they had accidents. In addition, the employer would eventually look for ways to encourage its employees and covered family members to be better drivers so they would have fewer—and less severe—accidents. The employer would be forced to implement automobile wellness!

The car insurance story is not real, but its applicability to health insurance is hauntingly accurate. This is exactly what has happened to employers and their employees. The large employers are mandated to offer coverage; the rating system links cost to the employee and family community; the participants are protected from preexisting-condition penalties; and the employer is left to try to figure out how to make people healthier to maintain affordability for itself and its workers.

Because employers own the risk for the health and resulting claims in their covered population, they find themselves reluctantly tied to sometimes-invasive wellness and care-intervention programs in an attempt to control this ever-increasing business expense. I refer to much of today's corporate wellness as wellness scavenger hunts: Employees and their covered spouses must check the boxes of their wellness-plan requirements as if they had found the items on a scavenger-hunt list. If the checklist is incomplete, the employee pays a per-paycheck penalty throughout the following year. I did not really like scavenger hunts as a child, and I don't really like the scavenger-hunt approach to wellness as an adult.

Just because I don't like the current approach to wellness does not mean I don't believe that employers are in the best position to positively influence risk and population health. My company's wellness program required me to get a colonoscopy when I turned fifty. I am familiar with the cancer-screening guidelines and knew the procedure was clinically appropriate. The employer requirement gave me a strong financial incentive to follow through on the test I knew I needed. Thankfully, my colonoscopy revealed no signs of cancer. Others my age in our company have had precancerous polyps discovered and removed. In our company, we believe this type of financial incentive for personal wellness and screenings is appropriate. Other employers feel that employee wellness is none of their business. Employers must individually determine their roles in their employees' health and wellness.

Employer-Sponsored Recap

- More Americans get their health insurance through their employers than through any other source.

- Large employers are mandated by the ACA to offer health insurance.

- Health insurance inflation outpaces general inflation, and employers have shifted a disproportionate share of this cost to employees.

- The risk and claims cost determine the cost of health insurance for employers with more than fifty employees.

- The financial risk, administrative burden, and employee-relations damage of health insurance have employers starting to question their role in the future.

What's Next?

Frustration over uncontrollable cost increases, increasing administrative burdens, and employee-relations damage from annual health insurance changes and wellness requirements has some employers looking for an exit door. Continued cost increases will drive employers to explore alternatives to the current options. These options could include public-plan options, Medicare indexing, or 401(k)-like defined-contribution plans, in which employers escape their current underwriting community cost burden.

Sources

(1) Congressional Budget Office. Table 1-1 Health Insurance Coverage, 2019–2029. "Federal Subsidies for Health Insurance Coverage for People Under Age 65: 2019 to 2029." Cbo.gov. May 2019.

(2) Christopher Girod, Susan Hart, David Liner, Thomas Snook, and Scott Weltz. "2019 Milliman Medical Index." Milliman.com. July 25, 2019.

(3) Christopher Girod, Susan Hart, and Scott Weltz. Figure 8. "2017 Milliman Medical Index." Milliman.com. May 16, 2017.

(4) Milliman, Inc. Figure 9. "2007 Milliman Medical Index." Milliman com. May 1, 2007.

(5) Department of Labor. "Report to Congress: Annual Report on Self-Insured Group Health Plans." March 2018.

Chapter 4:

ABCs of the ACA

THE ACA IS SOMETIMES REFERRED to as healthcare reform, but it is really health insurance reform. Public opinions on the ACA are split along party lines: The majority of Democrats have a positive opinion of the law, and the majority of Republicans maintain a negative perception of Obamacare.

Opinions regarding the ACA have not changed much over time. According to a Kaiser Family Foundation survey, 46% of Americans held a generally favorable view of the ACA one month after its signing in April 2010, while 40% held a negative view. Nine years later, the generally favorable polling results have not changed: 46% view it favorably, and 40% generally view it negatively. (1)

My sense is that those on the right feel the ACA is a form of government overreach that has made healthcare more complicated and more expensive, but they probably lack the specific details to support this opinion. My sense is also that those on the left feel the ACA expanded coverage and beat up the insurance companies for their profit-motivated denial of coverage and care. They probably also lack specific details to support their opinions. I understand that opinions fall along party lines, but I wonder how folks on either side

VIEW OF THE ACA BY PARTY

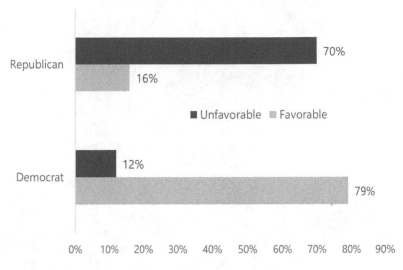

Source: Kaiser Family Foundation. "KFF Health Tracking Poll: Public Views of the ACA." Kff.org. June 18, 2019.

would answer this question: "So what exactly did the Affordable Care Act do that makes you like or dislike it so much?"

This chapter—and this book, for that matter—likely will not have any impact on your like or dislike of the ACA. However, it is vitally important for voters to understand exactly what the ACA did and did not do, and how the ACA has or has not been funded. Repealing, repairing, or replacing the ACA makes no sense if you don't know exactly what you are trying to fix.

I describe the ACA's biggest impact in the form of a three-ring circus. I don't do this because I think the ACA is a circus, but it is an easy way for me to communicate these three distinct, specific outcomes of the ACA:

- **Reformed Insurance Rules**—The ACA completely changed the pricing and underwriting rules for individual and small-group coverage. Insurance companies can no longer use gender in underwriting. The cost difference between young adults and older adults was compressed. Underwriting based on individual healthcare status was outlawed, so full preexisting-condition protection applied in all coverage. Insurance companies had to refund plan participants a portion of their premium if a specified percentage of total cost was not spent on claims. Plan designs in the individual market had to align with one of four metallic plan designs. Annual and lifetime benefit maximums were eliminated. The ACA completely rewrote the rules of the insurance business into a heavily regulated market.

- **Decreased Number of Uninsured Americans**—The ACA decreased the number of uninsured Americans by expanding Medicaid eligibility, creating a subsidized system for individual insurance, mandating that individuals purchase health insurance or pay a penalty to the IRS, and mandating that large employers offer health insurance to their employees. The result of the ACA coverage expansion is that the number of uninsured Americans dropped from an estimated forty-five million in 2009 to more than twenty-seven million in 2018. (2)

- **Sustained Medicare**—The ACA impact on Medicare is not frequently discussed. The ACA added new Medicare taxes and reduced scheduled payments to hospitals, home-healthcare, and skilled-nursing facilities. The combination of new revenue and decreased expenses increased the lifespan of the Medicare Hospital Insurance trust fund. The 2009 Medicare Trustee Report, in the year prior to the passage of the ACA, projected that the Medicare Hospital Insurance trust fund would be exhausted in 2017, but that trust fund has remained solvent, and the 2019 Medicare Trustee Report projects that the fund will remain solvent until 2026. (3,4) In effect, the ACA

Medicare reimbursement reductions and new taxes added nine years to Medicare's solvency. The changes were not a permanent solution, but they did provide temporary relief to Medicare's financial stress. The reimbursement reductions were targeted primarily at hospital and skilled-nursing facilities; the new taxes were aimed primarily at investment income and the wealthy.

The ACA decreased the number of uninsured Americans, but it came up well short of providing universal health coverage. Medicare delayed the insolvency of its hospital insurance trust fund, but the long-term Medicare funding challenges remain very relevant. The health insurance industry operates under a very different set of rules now than prior to the ACA, but health insurance remains the most complicated consumer industry in the world, and health insurance inflation has continued to outpace both general inflation and earnings.

Exchange, Marketplace, and Subsidies

The ACA created a regulated individual insurance program for federally subsidized health insurance that was initially called the Exchange. It is now officially named the Health Insurance Marketplace. The terms *exchange*, *marketplace*, and *Obamacare* are sometimes used to describe the same regulated and subsidized individual health insurance marketplace. By 2018, the number of people purchasing subsidized coverage through the Health Insurance Marketplace had grown to over 9.7 million. Actual enrollment was less than half of the CBO's predicted 24 million by 2018 when the law was passed in 2010. (5)

The ACA created a subsidy system based on income. Subsidies are available for individuals in households with income between 100% and 400% of the FPL who are not eligible for Medicaid or for affordable employer-sponsored health insurance. The percentage of income required for baseline coverage begins at 2.08% of household income at the bottom of the scale and rises to 9.86% for those at or above 250% of the FPL; 400% of the FPL is $49,960 for a single-person household and $103,000 for a family of four in 2019.

An individual cannot choose between Medicaid, employer coverage, or subsidized Marketplace coverage. Eligibility for either Medicaid or affordable employer coverage disqualifies the individual for a subsidy. Within an employer-sponsored plan, "affordable" means 9.86% of household income for *single* coverage; there is no affordability measurement for family coverage. Family members can get stuck with high-cost coverage through a spouse or parent but not be eligible for a subsidy because the employee-only coverage option is deemed affordable. In other words, affordable employee-only coverage can disqualify the rest of the family for a subsidy in the ACA Marketplace.

The subsidy amount is determined based on the cost of a benchmark plan, but the Marketplace allows participants to use their subsidies to purchase any plan available. The average per-person annual subsidy in 2018 was $6,600. (6)

2018 MARKETPLACE HEALTH INSURANCE ANNUAL AVERAGE

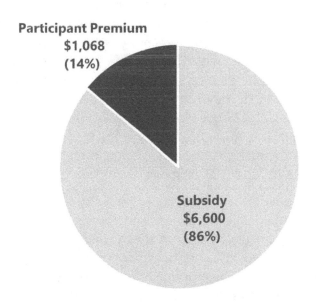

Participant Premium
$1,068
(14%)

Subsidy
$6,600
(86%)

Source: Centers for Medicare and Medicaid Services. "Health Insurance Exchanges 2018 Open Enrollment Period Final Report." Cms.gov. April 3, 2018.

What Does the ACA Cost Taxpayers?

Short answer: $1.9 trillion. (7) The CBO scored the cost of the ACA when the law was passed and continued to track its coverage and cost impact into 2017. The ACA has now been integrated into the broader review of federal government spending on healthcare, so there are no longer dedicated budget estimates for it. The CBO uses a ten-year economic-impact cost basis. The final CBO estimate from the January 2017 report is a cost of $998 billion for Medicaid expansion and $919 billion for the subsidized Marketplace system created by the ACA, for a total coverage expansion cost of over $1.9 trillion.

The ACA expanded coverage to approximately twenty million people. Rounding the cost to $2 trillion over a ten-year period equates to an annual health insurance expansion cost of approximately $10,000 per covered person per year.

How Is (and Is Not) the ACA Funded?

The largest source of funding for the ACA was from Medicare. The combination of Medicare provider-reimbursement reductions and the Medicare taxes provided Medicare with a temporary reprieve from its ominous financial position. This temporary reduction in the Medicare shortfall provided budget room to add new programs. You may be asking yourself, "Wait. Medicare is going to need all the revenue and savings it can get. How can the new ACA programs get their funding from Medicare?" Your question is valid. Although the original ACA scoring gave the ACA the dollars from Medicare savings, the programs are now financed separately, and there are no Medicare savings available to fund ACA coverage expansion.

The second area of funding was new industry fees charged to the pharmaceutical, medical-device, health-insurance, and tanning-booth industries. These are referred to as fees rather than taxes because the fees are not linked to or contingent upon profit but are applied based on market share. These industry fees have created significant pushback from the industries impacted who say that the fees simply increase the cost for consumers. With annual moratoriums, the industry fees have been sporadically applied.

The third area of funding was related to mandates and penalties. Large employers, defined as having at least fifty full-time employees, were required to offer health insurance to their full-time employees or make a shared-responsibility payment for not offering coverage. In a similar fashion, every American is required by the ACA to have health insurance coverage. Those who chose to not have coverage were subject to a shared-responsibility payment. The shared-responsibility payment for individuals was lowered to zero by the Trump administration and Republican Congress. The law still requires every American to have health insurance, but there is no financial penalty for noncompliance. The large-employer shared-responsibility payment implementation was delayed but is still in place.

Two major funding sources have never been implemented. A program known as the Cadillac tax was intended to create a 40% surcharge, or tax, on high-value health plans. *High value* was really just *high cost* because the tax would apply to plans above a specified total cost threshold and had no direct connection with the actual value of a plan design. The Cadillac tax is one thing in Washington, DC, that actually brings Republicans and Democrats together; both think the Cadillac tax is a bad idea. In July 2019, the House of Representatives voted 419–6 to repeal the Cadillac tax. The repeal of the tax is estimated to cost the government over $196 billion. (8) It appears that Republicans and Democrats can also agree that increasing the deficit is easier than confronting healthcare's cost and funding challenges.

The other unimplemented area of funding was a government-created long-term care program called CLASS. Actuarial analysis of the program showed the plan was not financially viable, so CLASS was quietly killed before it ever became a reality.

The ACA funding sources created, implemented, and that survived total less than $0.4 trillion in true funding. This is less than 20 cents of revenue to cover every dollar of new federal government expense for the ACA coverage expansions. The net result is an unfunded expense of $1.5 trillion, according to the CBO's latest calculation. (9)

What About Trumpcare?

President Donald Trump campaigned on the promise to repeal and replace Obamacare, but he left the task of developing and defining the replacement to Republican representatives and senators. Republicans and President Trump failed at their attempts to repeal the ACA, despite having control of the House of Representatives, Senate, and the White House. I have never viewed healthcare as a top priority for the Trump administration, but there has been meaningful activity that I can define as Trumpcare:

- **Elimination of the Individual Mandate**—The Trump administration was not successful in repealing the ACA and its mandate that individuals must have health insurance. However, it was able to reduce the penalty for not having coverage to $0. It is still federal law that Americans must have health insurance, but the penalty is $0. Trump supporters view this action positively as a removal of a government overreach policy, and Trump detractors view it negatively because it is expected to increase the number of Americans who do not have health insurance.

- **Stabilization of Obamacare Cost and Choice**—The Trump administration defunded plan-design subsidy payments to insurance companies in the Marketplace. Insurance companies raised premiums for everyone to make up for the federal government's renege on its promise to pay. The result is that the insurance industry has become profitable in Obamacare with stable rates and increasing choice. President Trump's action inadvertently brought price and choice stability to the Obamacare Marketplace.

- **Increased Choice**—The Trump administration has attempted to bring more choice to health insurance. Regulatory support of association health plans was attempted but has had legal and market challenges. I believe the single biggest healthcare creation of the Trump administration is the creation of the Individual Coverage Health Reimbursement Arrangement (ICHRA). ICHRA allows an employer to put pretax money into an account that allows employees to purchase any health insurance coverage they desire. An employer no longer has to offer an employer-sponsored health plan, and the employee can purchase any individual plan on or off the Marketplace, or even a faith-based health-sharing program. It is truly the individual's choice. With ICHRA, health insurance can move from employer-controlled to simply employer-funded. In a piece of legislative irony, ICHRA is essentially an expansion of a program created by the Obama administration for small businesses.

- **Increased Transparency**—The Trump administration has taken meaningful steps to bring transparency to pricing within hospitals and the pharmaceutical industry. These efforts have been met with legal and advertising resistance from pharmaceutical and hospital industry lobbying groups.

ACA Recap

- Public opinion about the ACA is split along party lines.

- The ACA reformed insurance, extended Medicare solvency, and provided health insurance coverage to approximately twenty million people.

- The ACA subsidies cover an average of 86% of the total cost of health insurance premiums.

- Revenue sources dedicated to funding the ACA coverage expansions cover less than 20% of the cost.

What's Next?

Almost ten years after its passing, the ACA is still a mystery to most Americans, and their opinions of it seem to be based more on politics than on an understanding of its true costs and benefits. The reality is that the ACA does not truly satisfy those on the left or the right. The Republicans failed in their attempts to repeal and replace. Expect Democrats to be the next to try to replace the ACA with something that gets closer to the social-justice goal of universal health insurance. Major legislation takes major effort and major control. Unless a future election creates a partisan clean sweep, fixing the ACA seems more likely than repeal from the right or replacement from the left.

Sources

(1) Ashley Kirzinger, Cailey Muñana, Lunna Lopes, Liz Hamel, Mollyann Brodie. Figure 8 "KFF Health Tracking Poll – June 2019: Health Care in the Democratic Primary and Medicare-for-all." Kff.org. June 18, 2019.

(2) US Census Bureau. "Health Insurance Coverage in the United States: 2018." Census.gov. September 10, 2019.

(3) Centers for Medicare and Medicaid Services. "2009 Annual Report of the Boards of Trustees of the Federal Hospital Insurance and Federal Supplementary Medical Insurance Trust Funds." Cms.gov. May 12, 2009.

(4) Centers for Medicare and Medicaid Services. "2019 Annual Report of the Boards of Trustees of the Federal Hospital Insurance and Federal Supplementary Medical Insurance Trust Funds." Cms.gov. April 22, 2019.

(5) Congressional Budget Office. Table 4. Estimated Effects of the Insurance Coverage Provisions of the Reconciliation Proposal Combined with H.R. 3590 as Passed by the Senate. "Letter to Honorable Nancy Pelosi." Cbo.gov. March 20, 2010.

(6) Centers for Medicare and Medicaid Services. "Health Insurance Exchanges 2018 Open Enrollment Period Final Report." Cms.gov. April 2018.

(7) Congressional Budget Office. "Federal Subsidies Under the Affordable Care Act for Health Insurance Coverage Related to the Expansion of Medicaid and Nongroup Health Insurance: Tables from CBO's January 2017 Baseline." Cbo.gov. January 20, 2017.

(8) Daniel Uria. "House Votes to Repeal Affordable Care Act's 'Cadillac Tax.'" Upi.com. July 17, 2019.

(9) Congressional Budget Office. "Federal Subsidies for Health Insurance Coverage for People Under Age 65: Tables from CBO's September 2017 Projections." Cbo.gov. September 14, 2017.

Chapter 5:

Individual Insurance Market Basics

THE ACA COMPLETELY REDEFINED THE individual insurance market:

- Underwriting based on health status (aka preexisting conditions) was outlawed.

- Premiums are based on age, but the age tiering is now government-set, and cost of the highest-cost age band is capped at three times that of the lowest.

- Insurance companies must spend 80 cents of every dollar on claim expenses, or they must refund participants the difference.

- Plan designs must align with one of four metallic values: platinum, gold, silver, or bronze.

- Annual and lifetime plan maximums are outlawed.

- Each plan must cover a list of essential benefits.

- Rate increases require federal government approval.

- A refundable tax credit subsidy system was created to help individuals and families at less than 400% of the FPL pay for health insurance.

Put simply, the individual health insurance market is now completely regulated. Benefits, underwriting, and rates are all regulated. Every American can now buy individual health insurance without the worry of preexisting-condition limitations, but the affordability of the coverage is still very much in question.

According to the Kaiser Family Foundation, 20,525,500 people bought individual nongroup health insurance through a variety of channels in 2017. (1) Approximately 9.8 million individuals purchased subsidized individual health insurance, and approximately 10.7 million people purchased individual coverage through any source without financial assistance.

Although those purchasing individual health insurance with and without a subsidy have the same plans available from the same insurance companies, the economics of their health insurance are worlds apart.

INDIVIDUAL HEALTH INSURANCE ENROLLMENT
(Million People)

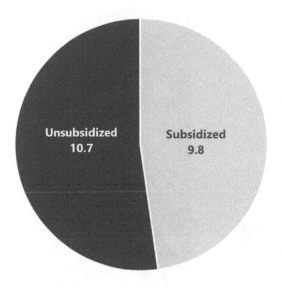

Source: Kaiser Family Foundation. "Health Insurance Coverage of the Total Population." Kff.org. 2019.

Nonsubsidized Markets

Inflation rates vary greatly among health insurance sources. According to data tracked by the Centers for Medicare and Medicaid Services, the inflation rate for health insurance purchased on a direct basis in the individual health insurance marketplace rose more than three times the rate of employer-sponsored insurance and almost fifteen times the rate of Medicaid. (2)

Those who are purchasing individual coverage using Obamacare subsidies have been shielded from these increases because the subsidies increase to cover the price increases. Approximately 10.7 million people purchase individual health insurance without government subsidy assistance, however. These individuals have felt the full economic weight of the health insurance cost increases.

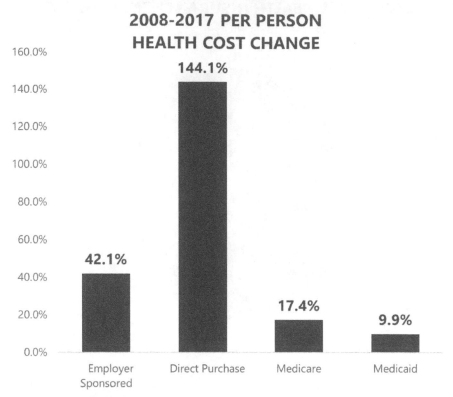

2008-2017 PER PERSON HEALTH COST CHANGE

Source: Centers for Medicare and Medicaid Services, Office of the Actuary, National Health Statistics Group. "Table 21 Expenditures, Enrollment and Per Enrollee Estimates of Health Insurance: United States, Calendar Years 1987–2017." Cms.gov. December 2018.

The Direct Purchase group in the chart represents the individual health insurance market. So, why did the individual market health insurance premiums skyrocket in comparison to other types of insurance? The elimination of underwriting rules and plan maximums has led to dramatically increased claims that result in dramatically increasing premiums. The health insurance premium rates for individual health insurance are the same for the subsidized and nonsubsidized participants, and the large claims and losses for the subsidized population are pooled with the nonsubsidized group. The biggest losers, when talking about health insurance premium increases, have been the nonsubsidized individual health insurance purchasers.

The largest premium spike occurred January 1, 2017. Even after insurance-carrier, provider-network, and plan-design changes, the average premium increased 21%. These rate increases caused many in the nonsubsidized population to reevaluate the value of health insurance. Health insurance participation among people purchasing nonsubsidized coverage decreased by over 20%. (3) Without financial subsidy, many decided that individual health insurance was too expensive and that they would go without it.

In addition to premium increases, individual purchasers face significant out-of-pocket costs. Consumer decisions in health insurance are very different when the consumer is spending his or her own money. Those without a subsidy choose a far less rich plan design. More than half of the nonsubsidized participants choose a bronze-level plan that has a 60% actuarial value, meaning the plan covers approximately 60% of eligible expenses. More than half the subsidized participants receive plans with actuarial values at or above the gold value, which covers 80% of eligible expenses. (3)

How expensive is the individual health insurance market? As an example, I pulled the following quotes for insurance for a fifty-four-year-old in Dallas, Texas, in February 2019. I selected a bronze, silver, and gold plan available from Blue Cross Blue Shield of Texas for comparison. Bronze plans have lower premiums but typically have higher deductibles.

	Bronze	*Silver*	*Gold*
Deductible	$6,000	$2,000	$750
Coinsurance (Plan Pays)	60%	50%	70%
Out-of-Pocket Limit	$6,650	$7,900	$7,900
Annual Premium	$7,863	$8,950	$11,343

Source: eHealthinsurance.com quotes for BCBS Texas coverage, accessed February 2019.

The bronze plan example costs $7,863 per year in premium and has a deductible of $6,000. A covered person effectively has $13,863 (the sum of the deductible plus the premium) of expense before the plan starts covering healthcare expenses. If the person is covering a spouse of the same age, all numbers are multiplied by two to get the cost for the household!

Rising premiums and increasing out-of-pocket costs are unfortunately not the end of the cost story for individuals purchasing without a subsidy in the individual market. They purchase health insurance in a discriminatory tax environment. Those who receive subsidies from their employers or from the government are not taxed on the subsidies they receive. In addition to tax-free subsidies, employees who purchase health insurance through their employers can do so with pretax contributions. Individuals who buy insurance outside of employer coverage must do so with posttax dollars. This discriminatory tax treatment effectively makes the health insurance cost for the nonsubsidized individual purchasing health insurance even more painful on the pocketbook.

Subsidized Marketplace

The ACA subsidy system was designed to shield participants from health insurance rate increases, and it has worked as designed. In a bizarre twist of math reality, the net cost of coverage for those who receive subsidies can actually *decrease* when the insurance premium rate rises. This happens because the increased premium increases the subsidy. Net premium rates for subsidized individuals have decreased in recent years. Yes, health insurance costs have decreased for Marketplace participants.

The percentage of Marketplace enrollees receiving a subsidy has increased to 87% of all enrollees, and the average subsidy has reached 86% of the premium. The significant premium increases created even larger percentage increases in the subsidies. The net result since 2016 is growth of 86% for the average subsidy and a decrease of 18% in the net cost paid by participants. (4–6)

MARKETPLACE SUBSIDIES AND NET PREMIUMS

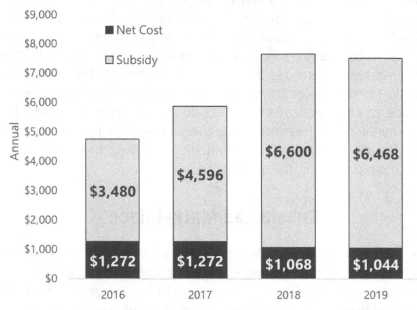

Sources: Centers for Medicare and Medicaid Services. "Health Insurance Exchanges 2017 Open Enrollment Period Final Report." Cms.gov. March 15, 2017; Centers for Medicare and Medicaid Services. "Health Insurance Exchanges 2018 Open Enrollment Period Final Report." Cms.gov. April 3, 2018; "Health Insurance Exchanges 2019 Open Enrollment Period Final Report." Cms.gov. March 25, 2019.

Choice

For those who receive subsidies, choice has been the big newsmaker. The news quieted down in 2019 as the percentage of people with three or more insurance carrier options increased, reversing a trend in decreasing choice. In 2015, 87% of consumers had a choice of three or more insurers, but by 2018, this had dropped to 45%. (7) Obamacare advocates were worried that decreasing choice could lead to a collapse in the Marketplace because of the lack of competition; Obamacare opponents used the declining choice as a signal of the ACA's pending collapse.

PERCENTAGE OF AMERICANS WITH THREE OR MORE HEALTH PLAN CHOICES

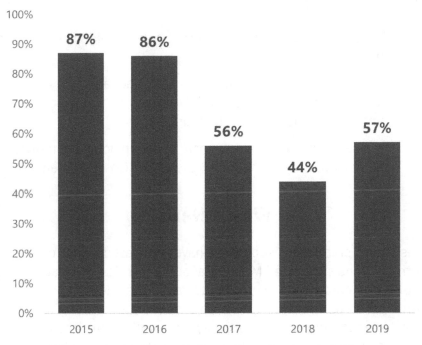

Source: ASPE Research Brief. "2019 Health Plan Choice and Premiums in Healthcare.gov States." Aspe.hhs.gov. October 26, 2018.

The uncertain enrollment, too many high-cost claimants, and congressional uncertainty around funding for Obamacare cost-sharing reductions created an unpredictable financial environment for insurance companies. Health insurance actuaries and underwriters like uncertainty about as much as Dracula likes eating garlic in the sunlight. Premium rates have increased to account for the comparably poor risk in the covered population and to capture the cost-sharing reduction funding within the rates for everyone. These dramatic rate increases have moved the insurance companies into a place of more predictable profitability. The improved profitability is resulting in increased choice for consumers. As much as it might frustrate Obamacare haters, many of the Trump administration's decisions have brought price stability to the ACA Marketplace and are helping to bring more choice back to Marketplace participants.

Individual Coverage Recap

- The ACA regulates the individual insurance market pricing, underwriting, and plan designs.

- Subsidized participants have been shielded from rate increases.

- Nonsubsidized participants have absorbed large rate increases and do not receive the tax advantages of those covered by employer-sponsored health insurance.

- Price and choice stability appear to be replacing the individual market volatility of the first years after ACA implementation.

What's Next?

Rates have stabilized, subsidies have increased, and choice is returning to the subsidized Marketplace. Democrats don't want to give Republicans credit for fixing Obamacare, so they don't talk about it. Republicans don't want to take credit for fixing something they were trying to repeal and replace, so they don't talk about it. Expect the moderate Democrats to push for a public-plan option, like Medicare, for Marketplace participants.

The unsubsidized individuals purchasing through the individual health insurance market face the most immediate pain. They need rate relief and are also looking for tax equality with employer-sponsored participants.

Legislators feel pressure to add choice to the Obamacare Marketplace. New options should apply to both the subsidized and nonsubsidized participants. Whether it is an option to buy in to Medicare or Medicaid, or the development of a public-plan option, the addition of a government-based option will be a hotly debated subject in the very near future and will be a key issue for these voters.

Sources

(1)   Kaiser Family Foundation. "Health Insurance Coverage of the Total Population." Kff.org. 2019.

(2)   Centers for Medicare and Medicaid Services, Office of the Actuary, National Health Statistics Group. "Table 21 Expenditures, Enrollment and Per Enrollee Estimates of Health Insurance: United States, Calendar Years 1987–2017." Cms.gov. December 2018.

(3)   Centers for Medicare and Medicaid Services. "Health Insurance Exchanges 2018 Open Enrollment Period Final Report." Cms.gov. April 3, 2018.

(4)   Centers for Medicare and Medicaid Services. "Health Insurance Exchanges 2017 Open Enrollment Period Final Report." Cms.gov. March 15, 2017.

(5)   Centers for Medicare and Medicaid Services. "Health Insurance Exchanges 2018 Open Enrollment Period Final Report." Cms.gov. April 3, 2018.

(6)   Centers for Medicare and Medicaid Services. "Health Insurance Exchanges 2019 Open Enrollment Period Final Report." Cms.gov. March 25, 2019.

(7)   ASPE Research Brief. "2019 Health Plan Choice and Premiums in Healthcare.gov States." Aspe.hhs.gov. October 26, 2018.

Chapter 6:

Uninsured Basics

A MAJOR GOAL OF THE ACA was to decrease the number of uninsured people in the US. The coverage expansions were implemented in 2014. Between 2013 and 2018, the number of uninsured people in the US dropped from over forty-one million to just over twenty-seven million. (1) Supporters of the law can claim that the number of uninsured people has dropped by more than fourteen million people. Those who believe the ACA did not go far enough will point out that more than twenty-seven million people in the US still lack health insurance coverage. So, who are these twenty-seven million, and why do they lack health insurance coverage despite Medicaid expansion, a new subsidy system, and a mandate that everyone have coverage?

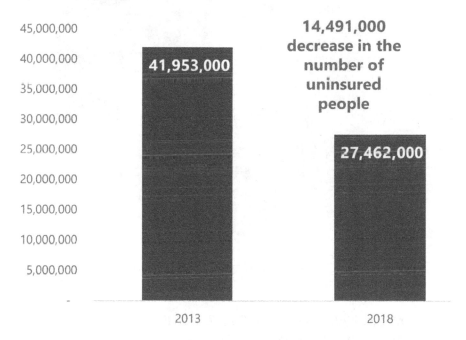

NUMBER OF UNINSURED INDIVIDUALS

14,491,000 decrease in the number of uninsured people

41,953,000 (2013)

27,462,000 (2018)

Source: US Census Bureau. "Health Insurance Coverage in the United States: 2018." Census.gov. September 10, 2019.

People

A 2018 report funded by the Robert Wood Johnson Foundation and the Urban Institute examined the characteristics of the nonelderly uninsured population. The report provides the following granular insight regarding uninsured groupings by rationale. (2)

CHARACTERISTICS OF THE NONELDERLY UNINSURED

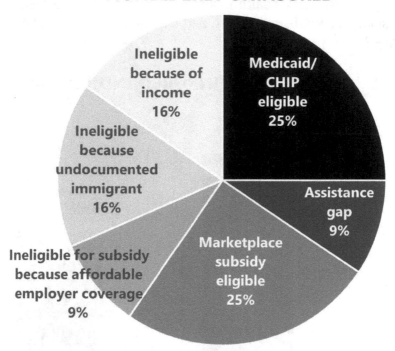

Source: Linda Blumberg, John Holahan, Michael Karpman, and Caroline Elmendorf. Table 2 "Characteristics of the Remaining Uninsured: An Update." Urban.org. July 11, 2018.

- **Medicaid/CHIP Eligible**—Over 7.5 million uninsured individuals are eligible for either Medicaid or CHIP. This group includes those who are unaware of their option for free health insurance coverage, have other barriers to enrolling in coverage, or are purposefully choosing to remain uninsured.

- **Assistance Gap**—This group of 2.8 million includes adults in states that have not expanded Medicaid eligibility and who earn less than 100% of the FPL. Marketplace subsidies are not available for individuals who earn less than 100% of the FPL; therefore, these low-income individuals do not qualify for Medicaid or for a Marketplace subsidy. This group is particularly economically vulnerable.

- **Marketplace Subsidy Eligible**—Over 7.5 million people are eligible for a subsidy in the Marketplace but have chosen to not purchase health insurance. The most common reason cited for this decision is that they still deem coverage unaffordable. The average subsidy covers 86% of the total health insurance premium, and the average per-person net premium is less than $3 per day.

- **Ineligible for Subsidy Because of Affordable Employer Coverage**—Over 2.6 million people have access to affordable health insurance through their employer but have chosen to not purchase coverage. "Affordable" is defined as a plan that meets the minimum essential coverage requirements and costs the employee no more than 9.86% of household income for single coverage. A worker who is eligible for affordable coverage is not eligible for a Marketplace subsidy.

  Family coverage does not have an affordability definition. The definition using household income and single coverage creates a potential gap for employees with family members. Single coverage might be "affordable," but family coverage may not be. Family members are not eligible for a Marketplace subsidy because the individual coverage for the worker is "affordable."

- **Ineligible Because of Undocumented Immigrant Status**—The ACA specifically did not expand coverage to undocumented immigrants. Hospitals are required to provide emergency care to anyone who needs it, without regard to citizenship or immigration status. For purposes of *The Voter's Guide to Healthcare*, I will not address this population. I view this as more of an immigration issue, and this book is intentionally not *The Voter's Guide to Immigration*.

- **Ineligible for Marketplace Subsidy Because of Income**—Marketplace subsidies are available to people who earn up to

400% of the FPL. Over 4.6 million Americans have decided that health insurance does not represent enough value to purchase, even though they earn more than 400% of the FPL.

Uninsured Recap

- The US, the country with the world's largest economy, has more than twenty-seven million people who have no health insurance.

- The ACA reduced the number of people without health insurance.

- Public programs that provide free or heavily subsidized coverage are available to many of those who choose to be uninsured.

- Gaps between programs create an assistance problem for some of the uninsured.

What's Next?

The bottom line is that the US is the only economically developed country without a formal universal healthcare system. This is a social-justice issue that cannot be politically ignored. Several states have introduced ballot initiatives to create universal coverage in their state. Finding the money within each state to fund the initiatives has been too much to overcome so far. Expect left-leaning states to continue to explore state-based efforts to achieve universal coverage if the federal government is unable to do so.

"Healthcare is a right" signs will be common in presidential campaign stops. If our country believes healthcare is a right, the question becomes whether this right has a corresponding responsibility—the responsibility to pay for it. The balance between the right to have something and the responsibility to pay for it, as an individual or as a country, is the essence of the political healthcare debate.

Sources

(1) US Census Bureau. "Health Insurance Coverage in the United States: 2018." Census.gov. September 10, 2019.

(2) Linda Blumberg, John Holahan, Michael Karpman, and Caroline Elmendorf. "Characteristics of the Remaining Uninsured: An Update." Urban.org. July 11, 2018.

Section Closing

If you had 100 people in the room representing a cross-section of the American population, the group would look something like this:

- 49 of them get their coverage through their employer and are concerned about rising premium costs and increasing out-of-pocket costs;

- 22 of them are covered by Medicaid, and more are joining the group every year;

- 14 of them are covered by Medicare, and more are aging into the group every year;

- 3 of them buy individual coverage with no government or employer assistance, and they face the full force of health insurance costs on their own every month;

- 3 of them get subsidized Obamacare; and

- 9 of them have no health insurance at all.

SECTION 2:

DIAGNOSING THE SYMPTOMS

THE HEALTH HISTORY FORM IS now complete, and the clipboard has been returned to the receptionist. The doctor now understands the relationship between Medicare, Medicaid, Obamacare, employer-sponsored health insurance, individual health insurance, and the uninsured. So, what are the specific symptoms? It is time to start the examination and do some diagnostic analysis.

The American healthcare system is suffering. There is intense pain in the pocketbook, severe bouts of confusion, and motor skill problems that are often disabling. Prior to recommending a course of correction, there must be some diagnostic testing done to understand *why* the patient is experiencing these seemingly unrelated symptoms. Proposing solutions without first understanding the root cause is like throwing a dart blindfolded. We must first remove the blindfold before taking aim at the target. This diagnostic exploration of the symptoms is our blindfold removal. Let's answer the simple question, "What is wrong with the American healthcare system?"

Chapter 7:

Pain in the Pocketbook

POLITICAL STRATEGIST JAMES CARVILLE IS credited with the creation of the famous political campaign statement "It's the economy, stupid." (1) If we asked Mr. Carville to create a political strategy related to healthcare, he would likely say the following in his deep Louisiana drawl: "It's the cost, stupid." The first, and primary, issue voters have with healthcare is that it is expensive.

What is the deadliest animal in the world? It isn't sharks, lions, tigers, or bears (Oh, my!), or even snakes or spiders. It is the lowly bloodsucking mosquito. The Discovery Channel does not feature an annual Mosquito Week, though, because the world's deadliest animal is boring, annoying, and seemingly everywhere.

Healthcare is sucking an excess amount of blood, or money, from our economy. It is draining tax dollars from federal and state governments, it makes our products and services more expensive in a global economy, and it consumes an ever-increasing share of household income. It threatens the economic health of the federal government, businesses, and families. I, therefore, refer to our high-cost healthcare situation as our health "costquito." Sure, it sounds like a lunch special at a Mexican restaurant, but the challenge and threat of the costquito are very real and very serious. The question is whether the health costquito is simply an annoying bug or the single greatest threat to our economic well-being.

There was a landslide in the 2018 midterm elections. No, I'm not talking about a blue wave or the Red Sea. Healthcare was named as the most important issue to voters in exit polls and received almost twice as many mentions as immigration and the economy, which finished second and third. (2) I was watching Speaker of the House Pelosi give her election-night victory speech when she awkwardly proclaimed, "Let's hear it more for preexisting medical conditions!" (3) I don't believe Speaker Pelosi really wanted the crowd to cheer for individuals' poor health status, but she knew the democratic focus on preexisting medical conditions contributed to the House of Representatives turning from red to blue in the election. Republicans had used the "repeal and replace" mantra to their advantage for several election cycles, and now the Democrats had found a way to use healthcare to their election advantage. It also meant she would once again become Speaker Pelosi rather than Minority Leader Pelosi, and she must have felt it was appropriate to give credit where credit was due for her promotion! Despite President Trump's attempts to make the election about jobs, the economy, or immigration, healthcare was the story of the 2018 election, and this was simply a drizzle compared to the healthcare flood that is coming with the 2020 election.

The White House's Costquito Problem

The federal government is the number-one purchaser of healthcare services in the US. Healthcare is the largest federal government expenditure. The federal government has been referred to as an insurance company with an army. Federal and state governments fund about half of healthcare costs and make 100% of the regulations under which healthcare and health insurance operate. The bottom line is that the federal government is inextricably linked to healthcare.

Analysis of federal government spending indicates that this characterization of the federal government as an insurance company just might be correct. Insurance companies provide health insurance, retirement income plans, and investment services. The federal government funds these services in the form of Social Security, Medicare, Medicaid, CHIP, Marketplace subsidies, and interest payments on debt. These insurance-like programs now account for the majority of federal government spending, but this has not always been the case.

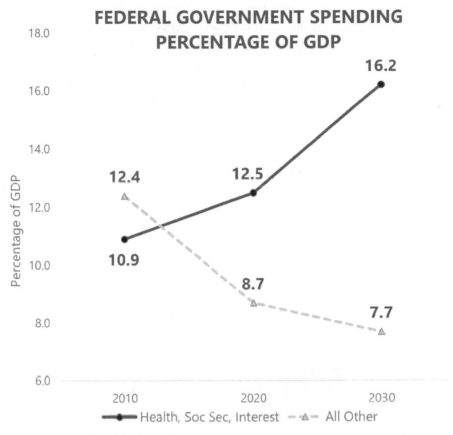

FEDERAL GOVERNMENT SPENDING PERCENTAGE OF GDP

Source: Congressional Budget Office. "The 2018 Long-Term Budget Outlook." Supplemental Data. Cbo.gov. June 26, 2018.

The nature of federal government spending has changed dramatically in recent years. As recently as 2010, all other federal government expenditures combined to top the insurance-like spending. This "all other" category includes things like defense, international diplomacy, transportation, education, national security, and healthcare research, among other things. Increasing expenditures on the insurance-like programs crowd out funding for these other important items. Every tax dollar shifted to healthcare expenses is a tax dollar that could have been redirected to other needs like education, infrastructure, defense, or public safety. High and increasing healthcare costs threaten other important government investments.

The insurance-like spending is fueled by the aging of the American population, healthcare inflation that outpaces growth in the economy, and government-funded healthcare coverage expansions. The spending pattern is projected to continue into perpetuity. Put another way, there is no turning back. Insurance-like entitlement programs are the primary business of the federal government. Therefore, the federal government can accurately be characterized as an insurance company with an army.

Healthcare, Debt, and Deficit

This shift in federal government spending might not be that big of a deal if government revenues covered government expenditures. The issue of the entitlement program imbalance is not just that future liabilities outpace future assets. Unfortunately, our country is spending more money each year than it collects.

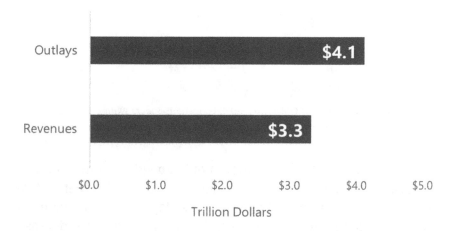

2018 FEDERAL BUDGET

Source: Congressional Budget Office. "The Federal Budget in 2018: An Infographic." Cbo.gov. June 18, 2019.

This imbalance, or deficit, means that future generations will be paying for benefit program expenses of today. In other words, a portion of the Medicare, Medicaid, CHIP, or Obamacare hospital or physician visit today will be funded by taxpayers in future years, and the gap is projected to widen based on future growth in entitlement spending.

How significant is our current public debt? It is not the worst ever . . . yet. The CBO tracks the debt held by the public both in real dollars and as a percentage of GDP. The combination of the Great Depression and WWII following shortly thereafter took our debt up to 106% of GDP in 1946. A strong labor market and economy gradually lowered the debt back to 23% of GDP by 1974. (4)

The recent combination of the Great Recession and the boom in entitlement spending has lifted our debt to its highest level since the end of WWII. The 2020 federal debt held by the public is projected to be 79% of GDP. (4) It is projected to surpass the WWII level in fifteen years and to continue an upward trajectory fueled by the entitlement imbalance. Debt spikes in our history have been connected to either wars or economic catastrophes, but the CBO future projection assumes no new wars or major recession and includes only the demographic insurance catastrophe. We are still near the bottom of the economic entitlement mountain, but no end to the climb is in sight.

FEDERAL DEBT HELD BY THE PUBLIC
PERCENTAGE OF GDP

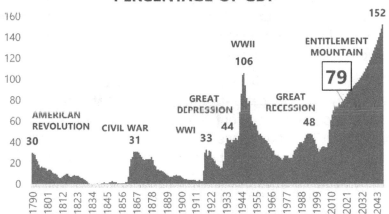

Source: Congressional Budget Office. "The 2018 Long-Term Budget Outlook." Supplemental Data. Cbo.gov. June 26, 2018.

Why is the growing debt a problem? Rising debt as a percentage of our economy weakens the government's ability to respond to urgent situations, whether they are environmental (think Hurricane Katrina), economic (think mortgage meltdown), or security (think 9/11). The debt weakens our ability as a country to respond with resiliency to crises, and it shifts money from responding to today's priorities to paying for yesterday's unfunded expenses.

From the White House to Little Pink Houses

The debt and deficit numbers can be daunting since it is hard to wrap your head around what 1 trillion of anything really means. One million seconds lasts approximately 12 days, and 1 trillion seconds lasts 31,209 years! When we speak of healthcare spending in trillions of dollars, it is hard to grasp how much that really is. Let's simplify the understanding by looking at debt and healthcare on a per-household basis. Instead of the White House, we will look at the Pink House. The Pink House represents the average American household and its share of the federal budget and deficit.

The Pink House family earned $25,864 but spent $32,134 in 2018. Unfortunately, the Pink House has a history of spending more than it earns in most years. The result is no savings and a debt of $123,452 for the money it has already borrowed to fund the lifestyle of the people who live there. The people living in the Pink House try not to think of how this financial pattern might impact their children, so they keep repeating the same pattern.

The family members have looked at their future earning potential to see if they can get better-paying jobs. Analysts are saying 2%–3% annual increases are about the best the future might hold. The income-growth limitations have forced the Pink House family to look at their expenses. Health insurance is their number-one expense, at $8,130 in 2018. This single expense consumed over 31% of the income. It is also the fastest-growing expense and has accounted for 60% of the net growth in household spending over the past decade. The owners of the Pink House have determined that health insurance cost is their number-one financial priority.

The numbers in the Pink House story represent every household's share of our federal budget, debt, and government healthcare spending.

The impact of healthcare spending on the budget and the debt is very real. The Pink House budget is further complicated by the inconvenient truth that the federal budget does not provide coverage for everyone. The majority of Americans don't get their healthcare coverage funded by the federal government; only approximately 35% of Americans get their health insurance through a government program. (5) In other words, our seemingly unaffordable government healthcare system only covers 3.5 of every 10 of us. That leaves over 200 million people, or almost 65%, who get their health insurance coverage through their jobs, directly from insurance companies, or are uninsured. The Pink House story does not include the healthcare expenditures for 65% of Americans. Expanding government coverage to more, or all, Americans potentially multiplies the debt crisis if we do not first address the underlying complexity and the cost issues in healthcare.

Pop Quiz

Please choose the response that best reflects your opinion.

A. Increasing federal budget deficits by knowingly underfunding current entitlement expenditures is acceptable because it provides needed benefits today without raising current taxes or cutting other programs.

B. Congress should not be allowed to increase public debt by knowingly underfunding current entitlement expenditures. Entitlement expenditure shortfalls should be funded by a required reduction in entitlement spending, by revenue increases, and/or by cuts to other spending.

The Little Pink House's Costquito Problem

For the ten-year period ended in 2017, healthcare costs for workers, including per-paycheck and out-of-pocket medical expenses, increased an average of 109%, while median household income increased only 22%.

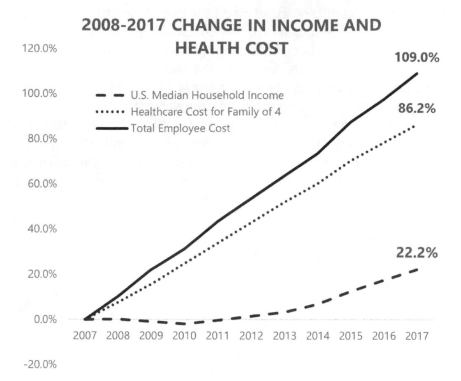

2008-2017 CHANGE IN INCOME AND HEALTH COST

- – – U.S. Median Household Income
- •••••• Healthcare Cost for Family of 4
- —— Total Employee Cost

109.0%

86.2%

22.2%

Sources: US Census Bureau. "Historical Income Tables: Households Table H8." Census.gov. August 2019; Christopher Girod, Susan Hart, and Scott Weltz. "2018 Milliman Medical Index." Milliman.com. May 21, 2018.

The US Census Bureau estimated the median household income at $61,372 in 2017. The Milliman Medical Index estimated the average total cost for health insurance for a family of four in 2017 to be $26,944. (6) The average healthcare cost for a family of four would consume 44% of the median household income in the absence of employer or government subsidy. Some politicians are promoting a single-payer system, but I think most Americans really want an "other-payer" system. This stuff is so expensive, they just hope someone else will pay for it. Without substantial employer or government subsidy, the health insurance cost is out of reach for the average American household.

Warren Buffett has referred to healthcare as the tapeworm of the American economy. (7) I refer to it as a costquito problem. Whether the parasite is hidden deep within our belly or is buzzing around our skin, the economic threat of out-of-control healthcare spending is an economic problem for the White House and for every little pink house in every community in America. Simply smashing the costquito in its economically bloated state creates a potential bloody mess. The right answer to our costquito problem is the one that safely decreases the flow of money over time.

Sources

(1)　Anonymous. "It's the Economy, Stupid." *Harvard Political Review*. October 17, 2012.

(2)　Benjy Sarlin. "Midterm Exit Polls: Health Care Is Top Issue for Voters." Nbcnews.com. November 6, 2018.

(3)　Shane Croucher. "Video: Nancy Pelosi Flubs Victory Speech – 'Let's Hear It More For Pre-Existing Medical Conditions'." *Newsweek*. November 7, 2018.

(4)　Congressional Budget Office. "The 2018 Long-Term Budget Outlook." Supplemental Data. Cbo.gov. June 26, 2018.

(5)　Kaiser Family Foundation. "Health Insurance Coverage of the Total Population." Kff.org. 2019.

(6)　Christopher Girod, Susan Hart, and Scott Weltz. "2017 Milliman Medical Index." Milliman.com. May 16, 2017.

(7)　Julia La Roche. "Buffett: 'Medical Costs Are the Tapeworm of American Economic Competitiveness.'" Yahoo! Finance. May 6, 2017.

Chapter 8:

Is the Price Right?
Underwronging and the Health Wars

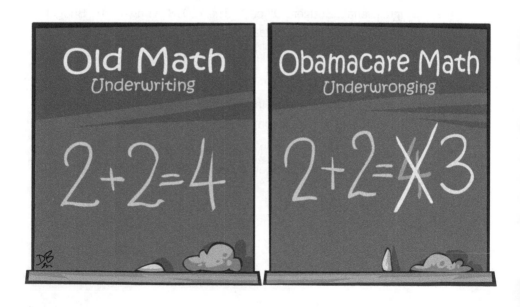

THE CONCEPT OF UNDERWRITING GOES back to the very roots of insurance. As ships began to sail between England and the New World, investors would sign their names under a ship's manifest, and so was born the term *underwriting*. The investors would receive a premium and would take a share of the loss if something happened to the ship and/or cargo. This sharing of risk allowed business owners to take the chance of sailing and trading in the New World. The balance between risk and reward is the basis of all underwriting.

The ACA created a system of under*wronging* in the individual health insurance market. Underwronging is the process of manipulating numbers because you don't like the answer that mathematics and statistics produce. The implementation of underwronging creates an almost insatiable appetite for subsidy and for continual manipulation. Just because the government mandates that $2 + 2 = 3$ in insurance, does not mean that 4 is not the answer in the end.

Insurance pricing is based on both predicting and pooling risk. Enhanced predictability leads to greater competition among bidders. The ACA outlawed many of the common health insurance underwriting factors that are used to more closely align risk and premium. Limiting or eliminating the following underwriting pricing elements created uncertainty for insurance companies:

- **Industry**—The health insurance of small companies was priced based on the common risk characteristics of the typical workforce in their industry. The ACA outlawed this practice.

- **Gender**—Young women paid more for health insurance than young men. Older men paid more for health insurance than older women. The health insurance rates prior to the ACA reflected the aggregate claims history by gender. The ACA made rates gender-neutral.

- **Claim History and Preexisting Medical Conditions**—Insurance companies could either increase prices or deny coverage for individuals with known medical conditions. The ACA outlawed preexisting-condition limitations.

- **Risk Factors**—Known risk factors, such as obesity and tobacco use, were factors in determining rates. The ACA allowed tobacco to continue as a risk factor that could increase premiums, but all other risk factors have been eliminated from pricing.

- **Age**—The cost of health insurance increases with age because claims risk increases with age. The rate and amount of increase may be shocking to the insurance novice. The claims risk for a sixty-four-year-old man is approximately 6.5 times greater than the claims risk for a twenty-five-year-old man. (1) Prior to the ACA, an insurance company's prices reflected the insurer's actuarial projection for claims by age. The ACA created a standardized age scale that applies to individual health insurance. The standardized scale caps the difference between the lowest-cost and highest-cost participant at three times the lowest rate.

The early years of the Marketplace have been defined by uncertainty. Uncertainty in insurance leads to volatile pricing, and that is what has been experienced. Insurance carriers were worried that the mix of unhealthy-to-healthy and old-to-young participants would not be favorable. The rate stability of the pool for an insurance company is based on the company's ability to accurately forecast risk. If a higher percentage of the enrollment was for older and/or sicker people, the rates would be inadequate and would become volatile. This is exactly what happened in the Health Insurance Marketplace. The national average monthly premium for the benchmark second-lowest silver plan increased from $218 in 2014 (the first year of the Marketplace) to $411 in 2018. That is an 88% increase in only four years. (2)

Underwronging and the Health Wars

Every political campaign loves to have a villain and victim. It sets the perfect stage for the politician to be the rescuing hero. Two fictitious "wars" have been created on the healthcare front: the war on women and the war on aging. We'll take a closer look to see if there really are weapons of mass healthcare destruction here, but before we do, let's look at two other types of insurance.

Life Insurance Example

The federal government does not mandate that any individual purchase life insurance. The federal government has not created a life insurance underwronging system, and it does not provide a formal life insurance subsidy system for individuals between 100% and 400% of the FPL. Preexisting conditions have a huge impact on your ability to purchase life insurance and on the rate you will pay. Life insurance is an actuarially pure business.

This may not surprise you, but there is tremendous gender discrimination in life insurance. Base life insurance rates for women are lower than base life insurance rates for men of the same age.

Wait! There's more. Life insurance rates also discriminate against older people. According to one life insurance insider, a healthy sixty-five-year-old man will pay over sixteen times as much for life insurance as a healthy twenty-five-year-old man. Somebody call Congress!

Age	Female	Male	Gender Variance	Age Variance
25	$193	$208	7.6%	--
35	$200	$215	7.5%	3.6%
45	$433	$440	1.7%	112.0%
55	$955	$1,305	36.6%	528.9%
65	$2,018	$3,603	78.6%	1636.1%

Source: Quickquote.com, "Women vs. Men: Term Life Insurance Rates." November 3, 2018.

Of course, life insurance rates vary based on age and gender because mortality risk also varies based on age and gender. On average, men die younger than women, and older people die more frequently than younger people. The insurance costs simply reflect the risk reality. There is no war in life insurance.

Automobile Insurance

I have two children who were born in September in consecutive years. The older is a boy, and the younger is a girl. I added each of them to our car insurance when they turned sixteen and got their licenses to drive. The cost increase for adding my son was greater than the cost increase for adding my daughter. Both were "A" students, and neither had had an accident (since they were just starting to drive). How could the car insurance company arbitrarily charge my son more than my daughter? It was purely based on gender. Talk about a war! The car insurance companies are waging a war on boys! Somebody call Congress!

I get it. Boys have more frequent and more severe automobile accidents than girls. Therefore, car insurance companies charge teenage boys more than teenage girls for car insurance, based on the historic claims they have seen from other boys and girls. Car insurance rates simply follow predictable historic claim patterns and risk. There is no war on boys in car insurance.

The War on Women in Health Insurance Pricing

I am not here to say that America has not struggled, and does not currently struggle, with gender, race, age, or other bias issues. I am confining my comments solely to health insurance pricing. Health insurance premiums have been included as a weapon in the war-on-women battle cry. The ACA eliminated gender as a rating factor for health insurance, and rates are now gender-neutral. Prior to the ACA, insurance companies typically charged women higher rates than men. This was particularly prevalent in younger adults aged 18–44. A ten-year study by the Office of the Actuary for the Centers for Medicare and Medicaid Services found that actual health insurance claims for working-age women were consistently higher than for men at the same age. (3) The average annual health claim spending for women ages 19–44 was 78.6% more per person than for men of the same age group. The pricing-discrimination question is whether it was appropriate to charge a group with measurably higher costs more for health insurance.

Any inclusion of the possibility of women paying more for health insurance than men as part of a war-on-women dialogue is inappropriate. The war on women in health insurance pricing was no more real than the war on boys in car insurance.

The War on Aging

The ACA compressed the age factors in health insurance pricing. The pricing of individual health insurance no longer aligns with actuarial age-based risk.

My analysis of individual health insurance rates prior to the January 1, 2014, implementation of the ACA underwriting and pricing laws indicated that in Texas, a sixty-four-year-old man would pay approximately 6.5 times what a twenty-five-year-old man would pay for the same coverage. These health insurance prices aligned with actuarial studies of health cost by age. The ACA capped the highest rate at three times the lowest rate. The net effect is that younger participants are subsidizing the health insurance cost for older participants.

ANNUAL PER CAPITA HEALTH EXPENDITURE

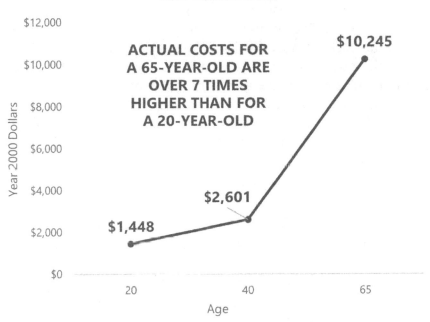

Source: Berhanu Alemayehu and Kenneth Warner. "The Lifetime Distribution of Health Care Costs." Table 3. Health Services Research. Ncbi.nlm.nih.gov. June 2004.

This rate manipulation creates potential instability in the health insurance market. Insurers must accurately predict enrollment by age, since rates do not align with risk. Republican proposals to repeal and replace Obamacare included a provision that would change the age-based underwriting ratio from the current 3:1 to 5:1. In essence, the Republicans were still supporting age-based rate compression, but they were splitting the difference between the 3:1 ACA ratio and the true 6.5:1 underwriting risk. Their thought was that rates that better reflected risk would be more stable over time and might better attract young participation. The result would have been lower rates for young participants and rate increases for older participants.

In my congressional district, a Democratic candidate for the House of Representatives successfully used an "age tax" ad as a key part of a healthcare ad campaign to unseat an incumbent Republican. The age tax to which the Democratic campaign was referring is the Republican-proposed move from a 3:1 to a 5:1 age ratio in individual health insurance pricing, under which older participants would be charged five times the cost of the youngest participants, rather than three times. The 5:1 ratio would lower the cost for younger participants but raise the cost for older participants. It also more closely reflects the actuarial cost risk. Was the Republican proposal to move age-based rates closer to actuarial reality a war on aging or a war on unsound insurance regulation? Healthcare is complicated. The ACA is complicated. The combination of a complicated industry and simple campaign sound bites is dangerous.

What's Next?

The government has permanently inserted itself in the manipulation of health insurance pricing. Any material moves to better align prices with actual risk would be politically risky. Young voters would be frustrated if they understood how the ACA-mandated pricing manipulation raised costs for them. A move to appropriately lower costs for younger Americans would raise costs for older Americans, angering the older ones. It is difficult to remove or correct price manipulation once established.

<u>Chapter Quiz</u>

Please choose the response that best reflects your opinion.

A. Health insurance prices should align with actuarial risk based on age and gender.

B. The ACA health insurance price compression to the 3:1 age ratio and for gender neutrality is appropriate.

C. Health insurance prices should better reflect actual cost by age but remain gender-neutral.

D. Everyone should have the same price for health insurance without regard to age or gender risk.

Sources

(1)   Berhanu Alemayehu and Kenneth Warner. "The Lifetime Distribution of Health Care Costs." Table 3. Health Services Research. Ncbi. nlm.nih.gov. June 2004.

(2)   ASPE Research Brief. "Health Plan Choice and Premiums in the 2018 Federal Health Insurance Exchange." Aspe.hhs.gov. October 30, 2017.

(3)   Centers for Medicare and Medicaid Services, Office of the Actuary, National Health Statistics Group. "Health Expenditure by Age and Gender, Table 27." Cms.gov. April 26, 2019.

Chapter 9:

Price Discrimination

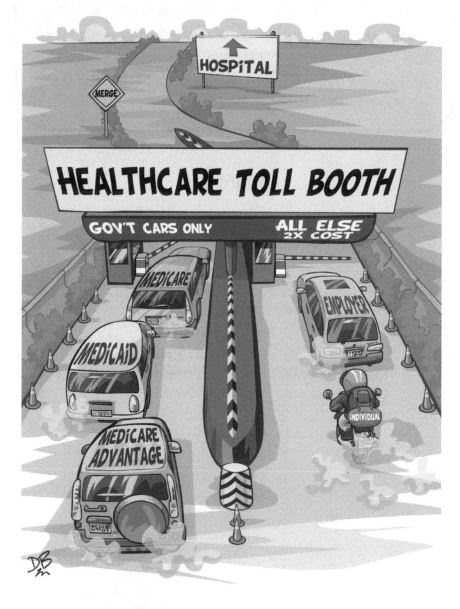

TWO PATIENTS ARE IN HOSPITAL rooms right next to each other. They check in and out on the same days. They are seeing the same treating physician for the exact same procedure. The only real difference is that one is covered by Medicare and the other by private insurance. After discount, the hospital collects more than twice as much for the privately insured patient. Is this okay? If so, how much price discrimination is acceptable to you?

"Price discrimination is a pricing strategy that charges customers different prices for the same product or service. In pure price discrimination, the seller charges each customer the maximum price he or she will pay. In more common forms of price discrimination, the seller places customers in groups based on certain attributes and charges each group a different price." (1) This is exactly how healthcare works. Hospitals group their customers according to the payment source: Medicare, Medicaid, uninsured, and commercially insured. This is known as payer mix. Profitability of a hospital system is often tied to effective management of this payer mix.

Payer mix matters so much in healthcare because the level of price discrimination is so high. Medicare does not negotiate with hospitals. Medicare reimburses based on its analysis of the cost of care, labor, real estate, etc., in a given geography for a specific procedure. Medicaid reimbursement strategies are set by each state and vary by state. Because Medicare, in contrast, is a consistent national platform, we will use Medicare as the baseline for this discussion.

Medicare Hospital-Reimbursement Methodology

Medicare uses its inpatient prospective payment system to set base reimbursement levels for inpatient services. The system determines the reimbursement by assigning one of over 700 diagnostic-related groups (DRGs) that adjust for patient age, gender, case complexity, comorbidity, and services. Medicare has been actively integrating value-based and quality factors into its reimbursements. The bottom line is that Medicare has a consistent national methodology for calculating healthcare service reimbursements based on its estimate of the efficient costs for delivering services. Medicare is a cost-based reimbursement system.

"The goal of Medicare payment policy is to get good value for the program's expenditures, which means maintaining beneficiaries' access to high-quality services while encouraging efficient use of resources. Anything less does not serve the interests of the taxpayers and beneficiaries who finance Medicare through their taxes and premiums." (2) Medicare knows it puts patients' access to medical providers at risk if its reimbursement levels fall too low.

In 2017, the aggregate hospital Medicare margin was –9.9%. (3) This means Medicare payments were less than the cost of providing the care. So, why wouldn't hospitals just stop accepting Medicare patients since the reimbursement does not cover the cost? Hospitals still have an incentive to provide care to Medicare patients because the Medicare reimbursement helps cover fixed hospital costs and excess capacity. Average hospital occupancy was 62.5% in 2017. Medicare helps absorbs some of the cost of excess capacity in the US hospital system, even though Medicare is not profitable on a stand-alone basis.

Despite the under-reimbursement from public programs like Medicare and Medicaid, hospitals in the US have maintained their profit margins because of the commercial reimbursement rates. This overall profitability has risen and been maintained despite declining public-program reimbursement profitability because the gap between what the government pays for healthcare and what commercial insurance pays continues to widen.

How Big Is the Discrimination Spread?

Three independent data sources indicate that hospitals receive almost 250% of Medicare reimbursement rates from private insurance.

1. Our company performed pricing analysis for a group of thirty-one cities in the Dallas–Fort Worth area. We found the most price-competitive networks were reimbursing hospitals at approximately 245% of Medicare for the total case mix of hospital services.

2. The Rand Corporation studied hospital prices in twenty-five states in 2017 and found that privately insured

patients paid 241% of what Medicare would have paid for the same procedures. (4)

3. A study of DRG 247—the code for the surgical procedure of placing a stent in an artery—in Colorado yielded similar results. The average billed charge was 576% of Medicare. The average commercial reimbursement after discount was 245% of Medicare.

Remember that the actual comparison to Medicare varies by hospital, procedure, geography, and specific network contract. What is consistent, however, is that commercial payers pay more than Medicare and Medicaid pay for identical services.

COLORADO DRG 247

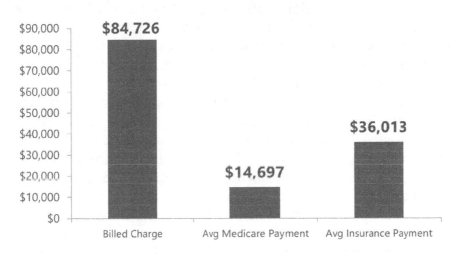

Sources: Holmes Murphy analysis of "2013 Colorado Hospital Price Report"; Centers for Medicare and Medicaid Services. "Inpatient Charge Data FY 2013."

How Much Discrimination Is Okay?

Employers are starting to ask themselves how much price discrimination is okay. The State of North Carolina provides an interesting case study in the effort to link provider reimbursements to Medicare. (5) The state was facing a budget dilemma related to the health insurance plan for employees. The governor has authorized an annual budget increase of 4% per year for health insurance, but the health insurance costs have been rising at 5%–9% each year, so state treasurer Dale Folwell chaired a committee to evaluate options to keep the plan solvent. The three basic choices were (1) have the governor authorize bigger increases, (2) cut benefits or increase costs for plan participants, or (3) lower the cost of the plan. The governor was unwilling to increase taxes or cut other services to increase the funding, and the committee did not want to simply shift more cost to participants, so Treasurer Folwell and his committee created the Clear Pricing Project.

The Clear Pricing Project was a shift from traditional discount-payment methods to a reference-based system that linked what the state paid for healthcare services to what Medicare paid. The initial plan was to pay hospitals 160% of Medicare for inpatient services and 230% for outpatient services. The plan was vigorously opposed by most hospitals in the state. Deadlines came and went, and hospitals refused to sign up to treat state employees at the Medicare-indexed rates. The state increased reimbursements to gain hospital acceptance. In the end, only 5 hospitals in the entire state—and none of the state's major hospital systems—agreed to the reimbursement that had grown to almost double the Medicare reimbursement rate. Treasurer Folwell said, "We've been exceedingly generous offering almost double what Medicare pays and yet not one large hospital would sign on—even those getting increases in pay. The fact is that transparent pricing terrifies them. Transparent pricing would end decades of secret contracts and high costs, causing them to have to actually compete for customers like any other business does in a free-market society."

The lack of hospital participation caused the state to give up on the Clear Pricing Project. The state announced in August 2019 that the full Blue Cross Blue Shield network would be available for state employees.

Treasurer Folwell's words indicate his frustration. Medical providers also expressed their frustration though the process. Frank Kauder, assistant director for Cone Health in Greensboro, North Carolina, sent an email to Treasurer Folwell that read, "Burn in hell, you sorry SOBs," in response to the new reimbursement schedule. (6)

I do not believe that Mr. Kauder speaks for all hospital administrators. However, there is strong resistance to linking private insurance reimbursements to a Medicare-based formula, even if the formula guarantees a much higher reimbursement than Medicare. Presidential campaigns are actively promoting Medicare for all, which would pay all medical providers for all services the same Medicare rate. At the same time, the market is feuding over a cap that is almost double what Medicare pays. There is a massive gap between what politicians are promoting on the campaign trail and in debate halls compared to what the market is struggling to implement.

What About Transparency?

Congress and the Trump administration moved the transparency system one step further by requiring hospitals to make their chargemaster prices for services publicly available. (The chargemaster is the hospital's retail price list.) The heart of this initiative was in the right place, but the coding complexity and sheer irrelevance of the gross billed charge hinders the effectiveness. What employers and consumers need to know is how much they will be charged after discounts, which typically exceed 50% for hospital services. The Trump administration is poking around with the possibility of requiring medical providers to make their real prices—the ones negotiated between them and the networks—publicly available. America's Health Insurance Plans, a lobbying association of large health insurance companies, is vehemently opposed to this level of transparency, claiming it would violate trade secrets. Maybe the problem with consumerism in healthcare is the fact that the real prices are veiled behind trade secrets!

Greater transparency in healthcare prices will not solve the discrimination problem, but it will lead to a greater demand for an indexed solution. Politicians should pay attention to this voter opportunity. Something's got to give!

Chapter Quiz

What level of price discrimination in healthcare is acceptable in your opinion?

A. **Unlimited**—Medical providers should be able to charge and collect the maximum amount that insurance companies and consumers are willing to pay. Healthcare is a free-market business and an efficient consumer model, and it should be free to operate as such.

B. **Capped at a Predetermined Percentage**—Medicare has a balance-billing limit for physician services for Medicare participants today. All medical services should have some level of balance-billing limit linked to Medicare's reimbursement to protect consumers. Healthcare decisions involve life, death, and pain. Therefore, healthcare cannot be a rational, efficient consumer model and requires some level of price regulation.

C. **None**—No one should pay more than Medicare pays for any medical service. Healthcare is a right, and medical providers are providing a social service that should have a socialized price structure.

What's Next?

Price discrimination is eating away at the earnings and savings for the 200 million Americans who don't have government-sponsored healthcare, and that's a lot of votes! Multiple bills in Washington, DC, are being circulated that would link the public and private reimbursement systems. The gap between what Medicare pays and what private insurance pays for healthcare services will decrease through either market-driven solutions or regulatory action.

Sources

(1)   Will Kenton. "Price Discrimination." Investopedia.com. December 27, 2018.

(2)   MedPAC. "Report to the Congress: Medicare Payment Policy." Medpac.gov. March 15, 2018.

(3)   MedPAC. "Report to the Congress: Medicare Payment Policy." Medpac.gov. March 15, 2019.

(4)   Chapin White and Christopher Whaley. "Prices Paid to Hospitals by Private Health Plans Are High Relative to Medicare and Vary Widely: Findings from an Employer-Led Transparency Initiative." Rand.org. 2019.

(5)   "North Carolina Health Plan Announces Network for 2020." North Carolina Department of State Treasurer. Nctreasurer.com. August 8, 2019.

(6)   Emily Rappleye. "'Burn in Hell,' Cone Health Manager Tells Health Plan via Email." *Becker's Hospital Review*. July 11, 2019.

Chapter 10:

Does Health Consumerism Work?

ECONOMIST MILTON FRIEDMAN IS CREDITED with saying, "Nobody spends somebody else's money as wisely as he spends his own." (1) The theory is that third-party reimbursement mechanisms, such as health insurance, create market and consumer inefficiency, leading to higher cost because the consumer is not the direct financial stakeholder. Republican healthcare platforms have embraced the Friedman theory of healthcare economics and almost always tout increased consumer responsibility as the cure for that which ails the healthcare system. The question is whether healthcare is truly an efficient consumer market where increased responsibility leads to lower cost and higher quality.

Consumer-driven healthcare plans (CDHPs) were envisioned in the late 1990s and launched around 2000. These plans were designed to pair greater financial exposure through high deductibles with web-based consumer tools. The consumer plans made the promise to lower cost and improve healthcare quality through empowered consumers. The landmark legislation for the healthcare consumer movement was the creation of the health savings account (HSA) in 2003. HSAs allow the employer and plan participant to put pretax money into an account to cover eligible healthcare expenses. The deposits can be invested to create a return that is also pretax. The HSA is the tax code triple play. Deposits are tax-free. Investment returns are tax-free.

Reimbursements for eligible medical expenses are tax-free. The HSA is the only item in the Internal Revenue Code that allows for tax-free deposits, interest, and distributions.

Why doesn't everyone have one of these tax-magic accounts? There is one hurdle that must be cleared to have an HSA: You must be enrolled in a qualified high-deductible health plan (HDHP). A qualified HDHP must have a deductible of at least $1,350 for single coverage and $2,700 for family coverage in 2019. In addition, coverage for treatment of an illness, injury, or condition must be subject to the deductible. Only preventive care can be reimbursed prior to meeting the deductible. This means no fixed-dollar co-pays prior to the deductible for office visits, nonpreventive prescription drugs, or routine care.

The term *high-deductible health plan* was not created by a marketing genius. Quite frankly, it doesn't even sound appealing. This is what you get with your HDHP: higher up-front expenses for healthcare, exposure to significant healthcare pricing variability, increased responsibility for personal health, and greater awareness of the Internal Revenue Code. It doesn't sound too appealing when you think of it that way. What the Republicans and the health insurance industry failed to recognize is the risk-averse mind-set of the American people.

Many people will overpay for additional predictability in health insurance. This buying mind-set and habit are not limited to health insurance. A 2004 *Business Week* study of Best Buy and Circuit City revealed that extended-warranty sales equaled 45% of Best Buy's operating profits and 100% of the operating profits at Circuit City. The profit margin on these warranties was estimated to be eighteen times higher than the margin on the goods themselves. (2) Best Buy and Circuit City understood that American consumers were willing to pay, and pay a lot, for protection against financial unpredictability. When they designed consumer-directed high-deductible plans, Republicans and health insurance executives missed what electronics retailers understood.

Participant financial exposure to increased deductibles has skyrocketed over the past decade. The increased deductibles are not limited to HDHPs but apply to all types of insurance. The average deductible was almost 2.7 times higher in 2018 than it was in 2006.

AVERAGE ANNUAL DEDUCTIBLE

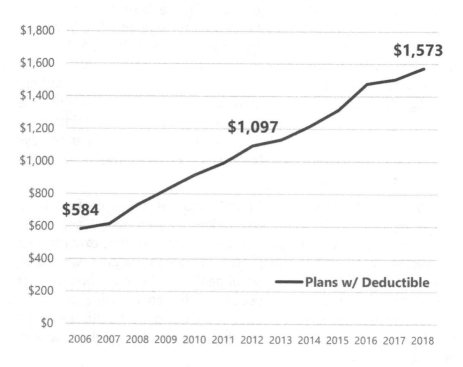

Source: Kaiser Family Foundation. "Employer Health Benefits Survey 2018." Kff.org.
October 3, 2018.

In spite of their higher out-of-pocket exposure, CDHPs have found a firm foothold in the market. Fifty-eight percent (58%) of employers offer—and 29% of participants in employer-sponsored health plans choose—a CDHP. (3) The lower premium price is attractive to both employers and individual plan participants.

The promise of the CDHP movement was not only that these plans would lower premiums by shifting to higher deductibles but also that the increased consumerism would lower inflation. Think of it like flying a plane: The altimeter measures how high you are, and the trajectory indicates where you are going. High-deductible plans lower the altitude of the health-plan cost by shifting more of the healthcare expenses to the participant. This gap holds reasonably steady over time. HDHPs cost $645 less per year than other plans in 2007, and they cost $618 less per year in 2018.

Unfortunately, CDHPs have failed in their attempt to lower the trajectory of healthcare inflation. The promise of CDHPs was to provide not just a lower cost but also a lower rate of increase over time because of better consumer behaviors. This promise has not been fulfilled and has turned into modern-day snake oil. The Kaiser Family Foundation Employer Health Benefits Survey shows that HDHPs produced a higher rate of inflation than the other types of health insurance from 2007 to 2018; the plans designed to shift costs to employees to slow inflation have demonstrated the highest rates of inflation.

Rise of the Underinsured

The dramatic increase in deductibles and related out-of-pocket exposure has caused a dramatic increase in the number of underinsured Americans. My simple definition of *underinsured* is the situation in which a person has health insurance but cannot afford the plan's deductibles and out-of-pocket expenditures if they have to use the insurance. In other words, they have health insurance but can't afford to use it. Underinsurance can create a very negative set of consequences:

- bad debt for hospitals and physicians,
- drops in personal credit ratings,
- patients skipping needed healthcare services,
- patients not filling prescription drugs,
- collection agency pursuits,
- consumers incurring debt to pay medical bills, and
- consumer bankruptcy.

In 2018, seventy-one million Americans had problems paying a medical bill or had medical debt. (4) Sixty-five million American adults per year have a health issue but do not seek care because of concerns over cost, and Americans borrowed $88 billion in 2018 to fund out-of-pocket healthcare expenses. (5)

NUMBER OF UNDERINSURED PEOPLE

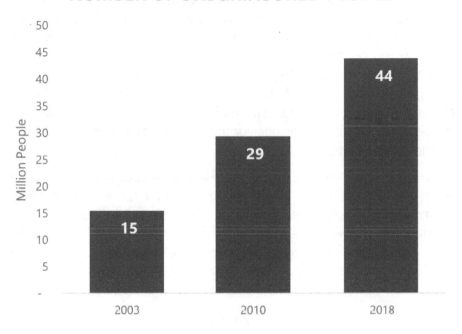

Source: Sara Collins, Herman Bhupal, and Michelle Doty. "Health Insurance Coverage Eight Years After the ACA: Fewer Uninsured Americans and Shorter Coverage Gaps, but More Underinsured." Commonwealthfund.org. February 2019.

The Commonwealth Fund has a more formal definition of underinsurance than my street definition. Its definition includes adults who had health insurance for the entire year but had a deductible of 5% of income or more and incurred actual out-of-pocket expenses of 10% or more of income or 5% or more of income if below 200% of the FPL. These numbers *exclude* any premiums for which the individual is responsible. The number of Americans in this unaffordable situation almost tripled between 2003 and 2018.

The effort to get consumer "skin in the game" has created some deep financial wounds for millions of Americans.

What's Next?

Does all of this prove that consumer-driven healthcare is a failed Republican and insurance-industry idea? It proves healthcare is not a perfect consumer market. When the choice is relief from unbearable pain—to take the medication or have a procedure that promises relief—what are you going to do? You are going to try what the doctor suggests. What do you do when you are told your child has a rare form of cancer and needs to travel to a specialist halfway across the country? You get on a plane to see the specialist, and you worry about how to pay for it later. The majority of healthcare *treatments* are for routine care, but the majority of *expenses* are not related to optional or discretionary treatments. The majority of healthcare expenses are related to catastrophic episodes or to complications related to chronic medical conditions.

Increasing out-of-pocket exposure is a dangerous game of roulette when the patient can't afford the treatment even with insurance. Lawmakers and insurance companies need to rethink how to better connect patients with the high-value treatments that give patients the best chances to get better. Insurance should connect patients and providers rather than put a financial wall between them.

Sources

(1)   Milton Friedman. "Friedman on the Surplus." *Hoover Digest*. April 30, 2001.

(2)   "Guaranteed Profits." *Business Week*. December 20, 2004.

(3)   Kaiser Family Foundation. "Employer Health Benefits Survey 2018." Kff.org. October 3, 2018.

(4)   Sara Collins, Herman Bhupal, and Michelle Doty. "Health Insurance Coverage Eight Years After the ACA: Fewer Uninsured Americans and Shorter Coverage Gaps, but More Underinsured." Commonwealthfund.org. February 2019.

(5)   Tami Luhby. "Americans Borrow $88 Billion Annually to Pay for Health Care, Survey Finds." CNN.com . April 2, 2019.

Chapter 11:

Do We Really Need the Pharmaceutical Border Wall?

THE POPULATION IN THE US makes up a little over 4% of the world's population. This 4% of the world's population accounts for approximately 42% of worldwide pharmaceutical revenues. (1) The US accounted for over 64% of the sales of new drugs introduced between 2012 and 2017. (2) People in the US pay more for many brand-name prescription drugs than people in other countries for the same drugs. The price-discrimination issue in the US ranges from obscure drugs to America's top-selling drug.

Turing Pharmaceuticals—The Extreme Example

Some blame the pharmaceutical manufacturers for raising prices. EpiPen's distributor, Mylan, was in the news and in front of Congress when the company increased the price by approximately 500% over a seven-year period. As bad as the press was on Mylan, it pales in comparison to the scandalous pricing scheme from Turing Pharmaceuticals. Martin Shkreli, Turing's CEO, received harsh news and congressional criticism for raising the price of Daraprim from $13.50 to $750.00 per pill. Daraprim is the brand name for pyrimethamine, which first came to the market in 1953. It is used as an antiparasitic and is on the World Health Organization's "Essential Medicines" list. The parasitic condition can be considered fatal without the treatment, which typically requires a ninety-day supply. Shkreli became known as the world's most-hated man and as "Pharma Bro" after he disrespected a congressional hearing by tweeting the word "imbeciles" afterward.

Despite the negative press and congressional pressure, Turing has kept the price inflated for a drug that has been on the market for over sixty-five years and is available as a generic in many other countries. The best price for a ninety-day supply of Daraprim in my sample city of Waukee, Iowa, on March 15, 2019, was $66,427.75 at Hy-Vee, and the highest price was $70,073 at a nearby Walgreens. Walgreens' price was actually above the $750-per-pill list price! Shopping around could save a couple of thousand dollars, but the price for the required ninety-day supply is still significant. As previously mentioned, it is a life-saving drug, so maybe $70,000 is worth it. After all, insurance will pick up most of the cost. Remember, Turing has no research-and-development investment in this decades-old medication; it simply has the ability to charge whatever it wants or whatever the market will bear. If you need this particular antiparasitic, then maybe the price sounds acceptable to you.

Pyrimethamine is widely available throughout the world. I checked price and availability from an online pharmacy in India, which had sixty-nine different versions of pyrimethamine available. The first on the list cost $5.04 when converted to US dollars. The $5.04 is not per pill but for the *full ninety-day supply*. (3)

How can US pharmacies charge $70,073 for a drug that is available elsewhere for $5.04? They can do it because the US does not allow drug reimportation and does not allow the federal government to negotiate drug prices. States such as Maine have attempted to legalize reimportation to reduce the cost of drugs for its citizens, but the federal government has shut down these state-based initiatives.

Humira, The Biggest Example

Prices for many brand-name drugs are higher in the US than in other countries. America's highest-grossing drug is Humira. The 2018 sales in the US for Humira were $13.6 billion and were more than double the second leading drug's revenue. (4) Humira is significantly more expensive in the US than in other countries.

ANNUAL COST - HUMIRA

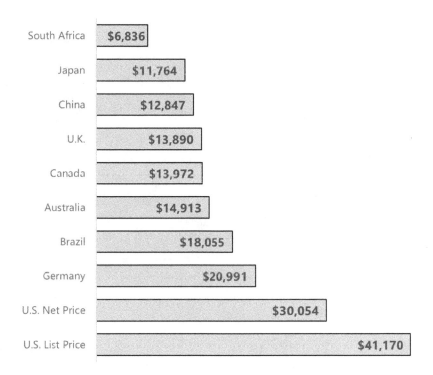

Source: Robert Langreth, Blacki Migliozzi, and Ketaki Gokhale. "The U.S. Pays a Lot More for Top Drugs Than Other Countries." Bloomberg.com. December 18, 2015.

Are these discriminatory drug-pricing problems the fault of the government, pharmacy benefit managers (PBMs), the pharmacy, the health plan, or the consumer? Maybe our high pharmaceutical cost has enough blame to pass around?

Federal Government

Many voters are starting to ask whether it is the federal government's fault for allowing the pharmaceutical system to discriminate against American consumers. Unlike other countries, the US has no centralized government entity that negotiates and sets drug prices. In fact, other than in the US Department of Veterans Affairs and the US Department of Defense, the federal government is prohibited from negotiating drug prices even for public programs like Medicare.

To make matters even more difficult for the cost-conscious consumer, it is not legal to import pharmaceuticals from other countries, even though the same drug may be available for much less. Think about the pyrimethamine example, where the drug cost nearly $70,000 in the US and $5 in India.

President Trump committed to try fixing the drug-pricing problem through an aggressive executive order. "We're working on a favored-nation clause, where we pay whatever the lowest nation's price is," said President Trump. (5) If this promise were to become a reality, it would dramatically lower drug prices for US consumers, but it would send economic shock waves through the pharmaceutical industry. President Trump's plan lacked detail. He did not disclose when it would be effective, how it would be implemented, or who it would apply to. The statement likely goes the way of repeal-and-replace or build-the-wall; it is a forceful sound bite but not a likely reality. The bottom line is that President Trump is signaling that the pharmaceutical industry's protections against government negotiation and drug reimportation are now on the negotiating table. Democratic presidential candidates are sending similar signals.

The pharmaceuticals industry is far and away the biggest investor in lobbying efforts in Washington, DC. (6) The pharma industry does not just have a voice in Washington, DC; it has the *biggest* voice. Ironically, the insurance industry holds second place in the "lobbying investment" category. Will the winner of the 2020 presidential election be able to speak louder?

Pharmacy Benefit Managers

Some blame PBMs for their spread pricing and rebate games. The difference between what the PBM buys and sells the drug for is known as *spread*. In addition to the pricing spread, there is a complex system of rebates that makes determining the real cost and value of a particular drug virtually impossible. PBMs are the middlemen in the pharmacy distribution channel. They sit between health plans, manufacturers, and pharmacies.

Some blame the potentially collusive merging of health insurers and PBMs. The three largest PBMs in the country are CVS Caremark, Express Scripts, and OptumRx.

- CVS, the owner of Caremark, completed its acquisition of Aetna in 2018, meaning the largest PBM now owns one of the largest health plans and is also one of the largest pharmacies. In essence, CVS negotiates the spread among all links in the supply chain.

- Express Scripts was the second-largest PBM and was acquired by Cigna in 2018.

- OptumRx is owned by United Healthcare.

The connection between pharmacy and health insurance could be an example of the fox watching the henhouse, or it could be the hens watching the fox den. Either way, health insurance and PBMs are inextricably linked in a massive game of vertical integration.

Consumers

There was a strong push toward the utilization of generic medications, a decision consumers ultimately make. A Commonwealth Fund study found that the US tied the UK for the highest use of generic drugs, at 84% of all scripts. This was more than double the rates for Australia and France. Consumers have appropriately played their part in generic drug substitution in the US, but our overall pharmacy cost is still high. (7)

New Zealand is the only other economically developed country that allows direct-to-consumer advertising for prescription drugs. In most countries, solely the physician determines which prescription should be prescribed. In the US, pharmaceutical manufacturers spend billions of dollars a year trying to persuade consumers to ask for their drug by name from their physician. Remember, none of these drugs are available without a prescription.

Is It a Price or a Ransom?

Disease can take you captive. It can disable you, cause intense pain, or even kill you. Disease is a criminal when it invades your body or your household. The insurance companies and the pharmaceutical companies are not the enemy . . . disease is. About a decade ago, an autoimmune disease known as Hashimoto's took me captive. I was cold all the time, gaining weight, completely exhausted, mentally dazed, and my hair was falling out. When I finally went to see my physician after my symptoms became unbearable, my physician quickly diagnosed the problem. Hashimoto's disease had attacked my thyroid and rendered it useless. Thankfully, I can manage the condition with a daily Levothyroxine pill that is available in generic form. I get my ninety-day supply at Walmart pharmacy for $10.00. If I take the drug, I feel fine and have no symptoms. If I were to elect to no longer take the medication, the condition would be fatal. My captor (Hashimoto's disease) has taken me hostage with the threat of death, but thankfully, the ransom is only $10.00 every ninety days.

What if the ransom for the prescription was $10,000 every ninety days? What if it was $100,000 every ninety days? I would pay whatever copay was required, and I would hope and pray my insurance adequately covered the drug. I got lucky that my condition is cheap to cover, but people don't get to choose their disease captors. When a disease takes you captive, you are much more of a hostage than a consumer; you will do whatever it takes to be set free. Maybe the federal government should consider managing the ransom demands? Pricing schemes that seem abusive to consumers could view the pharmaceutical industry rather than the disease as the kidnapping criminals.

Chapter Quiz

Please select the option below that best aligns with your belief.

A. The federal government should not negotiate drug prices.

B. The federal government should negotiate public-plan drug prices but should have no role in private insurance drug prices.

C. The federal government should negotiate public-plan drug prices, and private insurance drug prices should have a balance-billing limit that indexes cost to the government's price.

D. All drug pricing in the US should be negotiated by the federal government.

What's Next?

Should the federal government negotiate drug prices? Should the veiled world of spread pricing and rebates be brought into the light of day? Should the Food and Drug Administration start working on a plan to ensure the quality and safety of drugs imported from other countries? Should the price that Americans pay for prescription drugs be linked in some way to what people in other countries pay?

Prescription drug pricing will be a major campaign topic. Finding an answer that lowers cost while maintaining the level of quality control that Americans have come to expect and that adequately funds and rewards prescription drug breakthroughs is a monumental challenge facing Congress and the country. Lives and money are at stake.

Sources

(1) International Federation of Pharmaceutical Manufacturers and Associations. "The Pharmaceutical Industry and Global Health. Facts and Figures 2017." Ifpma.org. February 9, 2017.

(2) European Federation of Pharmaceutical Industries and Associations. "The Pharmaceutical Industry Facts and Figures, Key Data 2018." Efpia.eu. 2018.

(3) "Generic Drugs (3065) with All Their Brand Names." Medindia. com. February 2, 2017.

(4) Kyle Blankenship. "The Top 20 Drugs by 2018 US Sales." Fierce Pharma. June 17, 2019.

(5) Kaiser Health News. "Trump Promises 'Favored-Nation' Plan to Try to Lower Drug Prices but Experts Say It Wouldn't Move the Needle Much." Khn.org. July 8, 2019.

(6) Center of Responsive Politics. Opensecrets.org.

(7) Dana Sarnak, David Squires, and Shawn Bishop. "Paying for Prescription Drugs Around the World: Why Is the U.S. an Outlier?" Commonwealthfund.org. October 5, 2017.

Chapter 12:

Tax Discrimination

BOB BUYS A HEALTH INSURANCE plan through his employer from Blue Cross Blue Shield. The plan has a $1,000 deductible and $5,000 out-of-pocket maximum. Bob is able to pay his portion of the premium on a pretax basis. Not only does he save the income tax; he also saves his FICA taxes on the premium.

Barbara's employer does not offer health insurance, so she buys a health insurance plan directly from Blue Cross Blue Shield. The plan has a $1,000 deductible and $5,000 out-of-pocket maximum. Barbara pays for her health insurance with after-tax dollars.

Is it fair that Bob uses pretax dollars and Barbara uses posttax dollars for something the federal law requires each person to purchase? This is not a trick question. The obvious and easy answer is that it is not fair. The taxation of health insurance subsidies and premiums is inconsistent and discriminatory. Is that okay?

Largest Tax Expenditure

Before diving into the subject of the taxation of health insurance, it is important to understand a bit of Washington, DC, vocabulary. If I were campaigning for office and said, "I will reduce the federal deficit by reducing tax expenditures," what would I mean? If you thought I was going to reduce government spending, you would be wrong. *Tax expenditures* refers to money the federal government allows you to keep that would otherwise be theirs. These expenditures used to be referred to simply as tax deductions. Therefore, "reducing tax expenditures" means reducing deductions and increasing taxes.

Employer-sponsored health insurance is the largest tax expenditure in the Internal Revenue Code. At over $3.6 trillion over the next ten years, it dwarfs other tax expenditures, such as 401(k) deduction, mortgage interest, and state and local taxes. (1) Because employer-sponsored health insurance is the single largest tax expenditure, any government discussion about how to reduce the federal deficit and debt inevitably includes this issue. The tax inequity between employer-sponsored and individual health insurance makes it an even more desirable political target.

Why Don't Lawmakers Just Change Health Insurance Taxation?

So why don't lawmakers just make all health insurance an after-tax purchase and pocket the $3.6 trillion? First, voters don't like tax increases, and this one would hit an estimated 159 million people. It would also whack the workers whose contributions also become posttax, subsequently decreasing their take-home pay through increased taxes. If you said in your campaign that you cared about workers, small businesses, and/or the middle class, implementing this $3.6 trillion pot of gold may feel politically impossible.

Other employee benefits that receive favorable tax treatment have a cap on the deductible amount. For example, 401(k) and similar retirement income plans have caps on how much an employer and an employee can contribute. The employer-provided premium for life insurance above a $50,000 benefit for employees is taxed. In long-term disability insurance, either the premium or the benefit must be taxed. Employer-sponsored health insurance is the only benefit with no cap on either the employer or employee deduction.

Obviously, adding a new tax would be politically unpopular. However, there is another major reason that deficit hawks have avoided this potential windfall: The federal government needs employers to stay in the health insurance financing game. The tax-preferred treatment of health insurance makes it an attractive and efficient compensation element for employers. If employers drop coverage, the demand for government-funded coverage skyrockets, creating other budget problems. A major drop in the offer rate of employer-sponsored health insurance would negatively impact the labor participation rate, which would compress GDP growth. The potential collateral budget damage makes a move on the tax exemption for employer-sponsored health insurance a dangerous game.

If it is too politically sensitive to kill the tax-preferred treatment for employer-sponsored insurance, then why don't politicians allow individuals the same tax advantage? The simple answer is that tax-preferred treatment for insurance directly increases the federal deficit by further reducing tax revenues. Blatantly increasing the deficit is dangerous in a reelection campaign.

Is No Change Affordable?

The opening chapter of this book summarized the growing deficit and debt that our country faces. A fiscally responsible look at the annual deficits and growing debt would force a look at the government cost of healthcare and revenue linked to it. The CBO's "Federal Subsidies for Health Insurance Coverage for People Under Age 65: 2018 to 2028" paints a bleak picture of the federal government's healthcare financing. The net cost to the federal government after accounting for offsetting revenue is a whopping $9.25 trillion over the next decade. This number does *not* include the taxes, funding, and expenses for Medicare for people age sixty-five and over, which has its own solvency issues over the same period. It also does *not* include the states' portion of Medicaid/CHIP funding, which is approximately another one-third, or $2 trillion, more.

Net Federal Subsidies Associated with Health Insurance Coverage for People Under Age 65: 2019 to 2028		*Expenses*	*Revenue*
Work-Related Coverage		$3,725	
Medicaid/CHIP		$4,034	
Nongroup Coverage		$760	
Medicare		$1,049	
Total		$9,568	
Cadillac Tax			$47
ACA Penalties			$104
Health Insurance Tax			$161
Total			$312
Net Cost		**$9,256**	
$ Billion			

Source: Congressional Budget Office, "Federal Subsidies for Health Insurance Coverage for People Under Age 65: 2018 to 2028." Cbo.gov. May 2018.

Chapter Quiz

Please select the answer that best aligns with your belief.

A. The current tax structure that treats individual coverage different than employer-sponsored coverage is acceptable and should be continued.

B. Individuals should receive the same favorable tax treatment as employer-sponsored health insurance, and increasing the federal deficit is an acceptable way to fund the tax benefit for individuals.

C. Individual and employer-sponsored health insurance should receive the same tax treatment, and a cap that would apply to both is an acceptable way to fund the neutral tax treatment.

D. Individuals should receive the same favorable tax treatment as employer-sponsored health insurance, and tax increases or spending cuts to unrelated programs are an appropriate way to fund the tax benefit for individuals.

What's Next?

I don't like paying taxes any more than the next guy. However, the US federal government's support of health insurance coverage is fiscally irresponsible. Someday, we must face the truth of our healthcare-financing problem: The question is not *if* the unlimited tax exemption for employer-sponsored health insurance will be changed, but *when*, *how much*, and *for whom* it will be changed. The easy public target is the wealthy, so I anticipate the dialogue will start with capping the exclusion for individuals above a specified income threshold. That will be a start, but the issue won't die there.

Source

(1)   Congressional Budget Office. "Federal Subsidies for Health Insurance Coverage for People Under Age 65: 2018 to 2028." Cbo. gov. May 23, 2018.

Chapter 13:

Confusion and Dissatisfaction from the Most Complicated Consumer Experience in the World

NOT EVERY ISSUE RELATED TO healthcare is about money. Healthcare is also about people. Patients, consumers, employees, members, and voters are all the same thing, and navigating the healthcare system is a challenge in every role. Improving the customer experience is difficult when the customer is stuck in a vortex of confusion.

President Trump has infamously stated, "Nobody knew healthcare could be so complicated." (1) Several sources can confirm the complexity of healthcare.

President Trump obviously did not speak, for example, with the simplicity experts at Siegel+Gale before making this statement— or before the multiple failed attempts to "repeal and replace" Obamacare. Siegel+Gale conducts an annual survey and report to measure the simplicity—or complexity—of the consumer experience with industries and with individual brands. The study is called the Global Brand Simplicity Index. Health insurance in the US has been ranked as the most complicated consumer experience in the Global

Brand Simplicity Index. (2) This top complexity ranking isn't for just one year. Health insurance in the US has owned the bottom position each and every year since the annual ranking began in 2010.

Policygenius and Radius Global Research conducted a survey to determine how many people understood and could define the four key terms in health insurance: deductible, coinsurance, co-pay, and out of pocket. Co-pay was the most accurately defined term, with 52% of the respondents accurately defining it. Only 4% of respondents were able to accurately define all four terms! This may be even more shocking when you realize that 9% of Americans are employed in healthcare.

Confusion Leads to Dissatisfaction

Why do all this confusion and complexity matter? Because they lead to consumer dissatisfaction. The not-so-scientific opinion researchers at *Family Feud* have provided proof. I was walking through the room recently when my wife was watching *Family Feud*. I heard host Steve Harvey ask, "On a scale of one to ten, how satisfied are you with your health insurance?" The number-one answer was "One." It sounds like people were feuding with their health insurance providers!

A more scientific survey methodology delivers similar findings. The folks at the American Customer Satisfaction Index had the following to say about health insurance in the financial services sector: "Health insurance is, by far, the most problematic and least satisfying category in the sector, in part because it is also the most complicated and controversial." (3)

Gallup also reports dissatisfaction with the US healthcare system. According to Gallup, "Seventy percent of Americans describe the current U.S. healthcare system as being 'in a state of crisis' or having 'major problems.'" (4) The same report showed that 84% of Democrat or Democrat-leaning respondents felt that the US healthcare system was in a state of crisis or had major problems. This polling response provides strong insight as to why healthcare is a powerful political tool.

Surprise!

Surprises are fantastic on your birthday, but surprises are rarely awesome when it comes to insurance. Surprise bills may be the number-one complexity villain, and they have recently become the subject of media scorn. A surprise medical bill occurs when an individual believes they are accessing medical services from an in-network medical provider, only to discover that some expenses are considered out-of-network or are not covered at all. The RAPERs—an unfortunate acronym which stands for radiologists, anesthesiologists, pathologists, and emergency room physicians—have been among the most common drivers of surprise bills. These physicians sometimes choose to not join health insurance networks, even though they may be providing services within an in-network facility. The patient often does not have a choice among these providers and often never meets or sees them. The patient becomes aware of the RAPERs' out-of-network presence and service when they receive the bill long after they have left the hospital or medical facility.

I was working as a city's benefits consultant a few years ago. The city had an insurance committee with employees from different departments. The fire department representative was scheduled for knee surgery and became aware of the surprise billing problem through committee discussions. Prior to going to the hospital for surgery, he wrote "Cigna Doctors Only" on his leg with a Sharpie to make sure he did not receive any surprise out-of-network charges while he was under anesthesia. Much to his dismay, he subsequently received a surprise bill from a treating physician who was not contracted with Cigna.

Another common billing surprise situation comes from an emergency room or urgent care facility. Many plans include a fixed co-pay, such as $250, for an emergency room visit. This co-pay covers the emergency room facility charges; however, in many plans, it does not cover the services of an emergency room *physician*. To make matters worse, this ER physician may not contract as an in-network provider, so the patient ends up with a surprise physician bill that was not covered by the emergency room co-pay, and this unexpected bill might not even include an in-network discount.

Every Bill Is a Surprise Bill

The out-of-network surprise bills are a problem, but the entire structure of health insurance is a problem because every medical bill is a surprise bill. Neither the buyer (the patient) nor the seller (the physician, hospital, etc.) knows the terms of the transaction when a patient encounter happens. Unless the visit is covered by a co-pay, the patient does not know exactly what they will owe for the services received. The medical provider also does not typically know exactly how much they will be paid; they send in the appropriate codes to a third-party payer who either approves or denies the codes and applies their own calculation of total covered costs. Once the approved cost is determined, the third-party payer allocates responsibility for payment between the insurance company and the insured individual. The individual subsequently gets a statement from the insurance company and a different statement from the medical provider. Easy, right?

Until both the buyer and the seller know the terms of the transaction in a predetermined, transparent environment, confusion, frustration, and dissatisfaction will define the consumer and provider experiences. Simplicity must come to the health insurance transaction world despite the powerful forces of status quo that want to protect the opaque discounts world.

What's Next?

The opaque nature and transaction complexity in healthcare create a perfect environment for unpleasant surprises, which lead to consumer/ voter dissatisfaction. This level of consumer dissatisfaction creates political opportunity. Despite President Obama's "if you like your plan, you can keep it" promise, Americans are increasingly hoping for something better. The right answer to our healthcare-reform question is one that simplifies healthcare and health insurance and eliminates unpleasant consumer surprises.

Sources

(1) Kevin Liptak. "Trump: 'Nobody Knew Health Care Could Be So Complicated.'" Cnn.com. February 28, 2017.

(2) Siegal+Gale Global Brand Simplicity Index 2010–2019. Simplicityindex.com. 2019.

(3) American Customer Satisfaction Index. "ACSI Finance and Insurance Report 2018." Theacsi.org. November 13, 2018.

(4) Justin McCarthy. "Seven in 10 Maintain Negative View of U.S. Healthcare System." Gallup.com. January 14, 2019.

Chapter 14:

The Worst-Performing Healthcare System in the World

A *NEWSWEEK* HEADLINE READ, "HOW Bad Is the U.S. Health Care System? Among High-Income Nations, It's the Worst, Study Says." (1) Is the headline sensationalistic clickbait, or do we really have the highest-cost, lowest-quality healthcare system?

Upon first glance, one might believe this headline means we have the worst doctors, hospitals, nurses, technology, and training in the world. Is this what *Newsweek* was saying, and how is "the worst" measured?

Short Life Expectancy

Individuals born in the US have shorter life expectancies than individuals born on the same day in other economically developed countries—ouch! (2) This harsh fact is inescapable, but does it necessarily mean that we should blame doctors and hospitals?

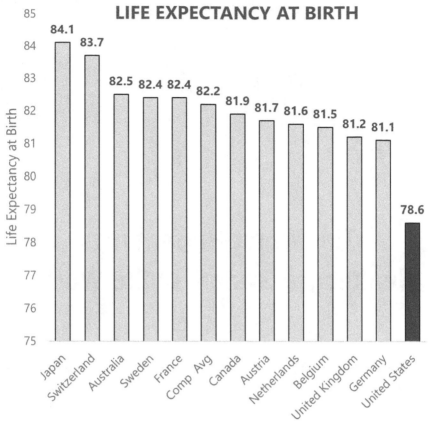

LIFE EXPECTANCY AT BIRTH

Source: Organisation for Economic Co-operation and Development. "OECD Health Statistics." OECD Health Data. 2018.

Measuring the quality of a healthcare system and the health of the population it serves is a monumental task. Life expectancy is a common measure, but it is impacted by many factors, with the quality of the healthcare system being only one. Can you really blame the healthcare system for social and lifestyle choices that impact this number? As an example, can you blame the healthcare system in the US for our higher-than-average rate of gun-violence deaths? Is the healthcare system to blame for our comparably high infant mortality rate, or do the obesity rate and health status of expectant mothers have something to do with it? You see, when it comes to measuring the quality of a healthcare system, it is very easy to offend everyone! Our social and lifestyle choices are sensitive political topics, so it becomes easy to default to life expectancy as a measurement and to blame the healthcare system for the result.

I believe the assumption that shorter life expectancy is directly correlated with the quality of the doctors, nurses, hospitals, technology, and training is far from truth. My mother is a three-time cancer survivor and the first woman in three generations on this side of our family to live through her early forties. Cancer prematurely took the lives of her grandmother, mother, and sister. The world-class care she received first at Baylor University Medical Center and later at UT Southwestern Medical Center, combined with the spirit of a fighter, allowed her to see children and grandchildren get married and to read this book today. Without world-class doctors, hospitals, and medicines, none of this would be possible.

Mick Jagger, the lead singer of the Rolling Stones, has the economic means to get care anywhere in the world. He had heart surgery in early 2019 at Presbyterian Hospital in New York. If the hospitals and doctors in his native United Kingdom are so much better, why in the world would he choose to seek care in New York? Mick Jagger and many others choose to seek care in the US because, in many measures, we have the best hospitals, doctors, and nurses in the world. If this is the case, however, then how do we have the worst ranked healthcare system performance?

Commonwealth Fund Rankings

The Commonwealth Fund has taken up the challenge of ranking healthcare system outcomes and compared healthcare systems in eleven economically developed countries through their report "Mirror, Mirror: International Comparison Reflects Flaws and Opportunities for Better U.S. Health Care." The Commonwealth Fund's measurement includes five categories: care process, access, administrative efficiency, equity, and healthcare outcomes. (3) The US was rated as the best performer in many healthcare areas. Providers do a better job talking to patients about diet, exercise, smoking, and alcohol risks. Specialists talked to patients about treatment choices and involved patients in decisions. Thankfully, the US five-year breast cancer survival rate was the highest.

Unfortunately, the US was also the worst performer in many important areas:

- Americans had more cost-related access problems.

- Patients were more frequently surprised that things were not covered by insurance.

- Fewer Americans have a regular doctor, and the variance by income level for those who have a regular doctor is higher than in other countries.

- The US infant mortality was the highest.

- Life expectancy at age sixty was the lowest.

- More Americans have at least two chronic medical conditions.

The bottom line is that the US healthcare system ranked last among the eleven countries overall in access, equity, and healthcare outcomes. (3) Our system is difficult to access and navigate, and it is economically biased. The result is that Americans often do not get the care they need.

Mortality Amenable to Healthcare

It is difficult to find pride in the last-place ranking of these important issues. Of particular concern is the last-place ranking in mortality amenable to health. An amenable mortality cause is one for which early detection or effective treatment could have prevented death. Translating this in a way my Texas public-school-educated mind can interpret, this means that mortality amenable to healthcare measures the rate at which people die from conditions that could have been discovered and effectively treated within the healthcare system. In other words, diagnosis and treatment were available, but people died anyway.

The US produced the most deaths per 100,000 people from factors amenable to healthcare—59% above the European average. Our healthcare system failed to keep people alive from conditions that could and should have been treatable.

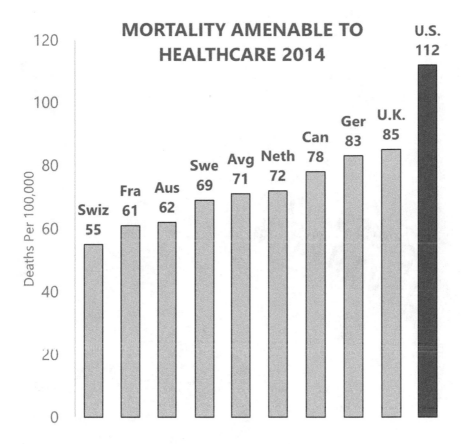

Source: European Observatory on Health Systems and Policies. 2017.

The finding that 112 people of every 100,000 died from healthcare system failures may not feel like much on the surface, but numbers and healthcare get real when they are personal. My definition of minor surgery is surgery on someone else. If it is my body that is undergoing surgery, then it is not minor to me. Applying the total US population to the Commonwealth Fund's study means that just over 1,000 Americans die every single day from findable and curable conditions. It becomes very personal if one of the 1,000 is a friend, coworker, family member, child, parent, or you. Whether the failure is blamed on the patient, the medical provider, the insurance company, the government, or some combination is not the point; the point is that the costly and complicated system is not working well, and it is killing Americans.

The T. Rex Effect

Except in the movies, the tyrannosaurus rex is long extinct. Imagine if there had been a prevention or cure available for whatever caused its demise. In my imagination, a "dinosaur survival button" is high on a wall or a tree. A simple push of the button can provide protection to the dinosaur. A tyrannosaurus rex, with its awkwardly short arms, walks up to the button, looking for help. The button is just above head height, and the short-armed creature is unable to reach the button. With the cure in sight but just out of reach, the individual dinosaur dies. Ultimately, its entire species becomes extinct because salvation, although available, was just out of reach. I call this the T. rex effect in American healthcare: A cure is available, but it is just slightly out of reach for those who need it.

Healthcare in the US suffers from the T. rex effect because the world's best care sits slightly out of reach due to a combination of cost, complexity, education, and other solvable factors. In many ways, we have the best healthcare system in the world, with some of the best physicians working in some of the best facilities, using some of the best technology and equipment in the world. Despite the great doctors, hospitals, and technology, however, people in the US die at a rate that is more than 50% higher than the average for other economically developed countries from conditions that could have been prevented or cured. Unfortunately, the T. rex effect is fatal for far too many Americans. The right answer to our healthcare-reform question is the one that removes cost and complexity hurdles to connect at-risk individuals to the care they need.

What's Next?

The focus of the healthcare-reform debate is on the component parts of cost and coverage. Questions of how much healthcare costs and who is covered dominate the debate. The result is worse than the sum of the parts; the result is an unacceptable mortality rate from conditions that could have been cured . . . the T. rex effect. A focus on the poor outcomes of our healthcare system might give us the courage to deal with a real answer to our component-part problems. Will any politician have the guts to transform and liven up the vision and debate?

Sources

(1) Ryan Bort. "How Bad Is U.S. Health Care? Among High-Income Nations, It's the Worst, Study Says." *Newsweek*. July 14, 2017.

(2) Organisation for Economic Co-operation and Development. "OECD Health Statistics." OECD Health Data. 2018.

(3) Eric Schneider, Dana Sarnak, David Squires, Arnav Shah, and Michelle Doty. "Mirror, Mirror: International Comparison Reflects Flaws and Opportunities for Better U.S. Health Care." Commonwealthfund.org. July 14, 2017.

Section Closing

The cost, complexity, and coverage issues are not independent problems. They are inextricably linked and all add up to our poor-quality outcomes.

SECTION 3:

TREATMENT OPTIONS

THE COST, COMPLEXITY, QUALITY, AND coverage challenges have combined to make healthcare the number-one campaign priority for voters. Complaining about the current healthcare system might get audiences lathered up, but candidates should be forced to describe and defend their alternatives to the current system.

This section of the book outlines treatment options to cure the symptoms of the current healthcare system for voter consideration. The proposals can be categorized according to political belief. The political positioning drives the beliefs regarding the amount of change needed to cure healthcare's ills:

- **Far Left**—Those on the far left believe the current system is irreparably broken and should be totally replaced with a government system because healthcare is a right for everyone. Medicare for all is the only logical option for those on the far left. To put it in medical terms, they believe a complete *transplant* of the healthcare system is the only option.

- **Center Left**—Those on the center left believe the ACA can be fixed by a further expansion of the federal government's role and influence in healthcare. The private healthcare system has failed in expanding affordable access to health insurance; therefore, the federal government needs to step in with public insurance programs where the private system has failed. Medicare for more, or similar public-plan options, are the preferred pathway for those in the center left. I would categorize their recommended treatment in medical terms as an *inpatient surgery.*

- **Center Right**—Those in the center right believe that the combination of private innovation and consumer engagement will lead to the most-efficient and highest-quality healthcare system. Quietly, this group admits that the coverage expansions and preexisting-condition protections within the ACA are politically popular and that the group can no longer afford to publicly fight against the ACA. Additional private-plan flexibility through things like tax-preferred accounts are popular with the center right. In medical terms, the center right recommends a *minimally invasive outpatient procedure* followed by a bit of physical therapy.

- **Far Right**—Those on the far right believe that the ACA is an unconstitutional government overreach into healthcare and that the ACA is a major contributor to our cost problems. If the government would decrease its overregulation of healthcare, then the free market would improve care quality and cost efficiency. "Repeal and replace" is still alive as a dream for those on the far right. Theirs is the medical equivalent of *take two aspirin and call me in four years if you don't feel better.*

Multiple approaches to transforming the American healthcare system are actively discussed and debated in Washington, DC, with influence from those across the political belief spectrum. Organizing the issues and options in an understandable way is a massive challenge for the voter who does not work in healthcare financing every day. The primary issues and options surround coverage, prices, and the role that government, employers, and individuals play in financing the system.

- **Universal Coverage or Universal Access**—*Universal coverage* means everyone has health insurance. *Universal access* means everyone has the choice and option to have health insurance. The ACA granted universal access—no American can be turned down for health insurance—but the ACA came well short of the universal-coverage goal, in which every single

American has health insurance. *Does the plan cover everyone, or does it give everyone the choice to be covered?*

- **Government Regulation of Healthcare Prices**—The government already regulates insurance prices and medical-loss ratios through the ACA, but the ACA did not address the price of healthcare services. Many currently debated proposals have the government regulating the prices paid to medical providers. *What role does the federal government play in setting prices for healthcare services?*

- **Single-Payer System or Public-Private Partnership**—In a *single-payer system*, the government acts as the sole administrator. As an example, the IRS is the sole administrator of the tax code. In a *public-private partnership*, public programs coordinate with private programs to create options. Medicare is currently an example of a public-private partnership, where 80% of Medicare participants have some type of private insurance to supplement or replace traditional Medicare coverage. *Is the government's role to be the sole administrator or the administrative foundation?*

- **Employer-Sponsored Health Insurance Stays or Goes**—More Americans get their health insurance through their employers than through any other source. Some proposals maintain some type of employment-based coverage to keep a sense of stability for working Americans and to decrease or avoid the need for new taxes. Others eliminate the role of employers rather than paying a tax to fund the system. *Should employment impact your health insurance coverage options, and how should employers pay for healthcare?*

- **Participant Cost Sharing**—Some plans have no premium or cost sharing; these plans often get described as free health insurance. All funding for these plans comes through new taxes and fees. Other plans try to avoid the full burden of new taxes and charge participants for coverage and care. *What is the appropriate and acceptable level of participant cost sharing?*

Chapter 15:

Medicare for All

REPUBLICANS FOUND A UNIFYING RALLYING cry in "repeal and replace." While campaigning, they were never forced to answer the question "Replace with what?" The fuel was resentment of Obamacare and resentment for the Democrats who had forced Obamacare down their legislative throats. The political campaign power was really more of a "repeal and *erase*" outcry. The voter response to "repeal and replace" was real, and it was powerful.

Democrats may have found their rallying cry in "Medicare for all." So far, they have been just as effective as the Republicans in not defining exactly what this means or how it would be funded. The term "Medicare for all" is as offensive to Tea Party Republicans as a MAGA hat is to Socialist Democrats. Medicare for all may or may not make it through the gauntlet of the Democratic primaries, but it is a poke in the eye to Republicans, as it proclaims not only that Obamacare is alive and well but also that Obamacare was not enough. Effectively, Medicare for all is the Democratic repeal-and-replace rallying cry, but what exactly is Medicare for all?

Medicare for All . . . Popular but Confusing

I will always remember the 2016 Bernie Sanders presidential campaign for one thing. No, not that a self-proclaimed Democratic Socialist who isn't officially a Democrat almost beat the most established of the Democratic establishment in the primary. I will remember how crowds reacted when Senator Sanders said, "Medicare for all," rather than "single payer." The phrases could possibly be used synonymously, but the crowd reaction is very different. *Single payer* sounds limited, restrictive, autocratic, and "governmenty." *Medicare for all* sounds inclusive, friendly, and safe. It literally sounds more American.

The problem with this branding is that Senator Sanders' legislation abolishes the current public-private Medicare program completely and replaces it with a single-payer system. Other candidates are now supporting an idea of Medicare for all that applies the current Medicare program as universal coverage for everyone. The Medicare expansion proposals also expand eligibility into the current Medicare system. Voters have become confused as to what candidates are proposing when they refer to Medicare because the candidates mean different things but use the same word.

An October 2018 poll found that 79% of Americans supported Medicare for all. This included 85% of Democrats and even 52% of Republicans. (1) The public appeal of these three words can help you understand why candidates rushed to support Medicare for all.

A June 2019 Kaiser Family Foundation survey asked Democrat potential voters about some key elements of Medicare for all, including whether people and companies would still pay premiums, whether people could keep their current plans, whether they could keep employer-sponsored coverage, and whether people would still have deductibles. The correct answer to each question, according to the proposed Medicare for all legislation, is *no*. The majority of Democrats incorrectly answered *yes* to each question.

WHAT IS MEDICARE FOR ALL?

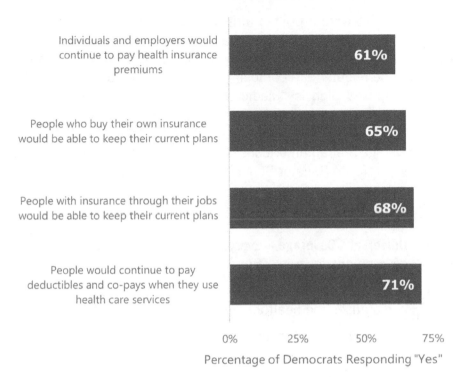

Source: Kaiser Family Foundation. Figure 6. "KFF Health Tracking Poll - June 2019." Kff.org. June 18, 2019.

Popularity of Medicare for all is dropping as people are learning more about what the term might, or might not, mean. A July 2019 poll showed that support for Medicare for all had dropped to 53% of all voters, and Republican support for it had fallen to 27%. (2) Although public opinion of the term is falling, it is still supported by a majority of voters.

Medicare for None

Senator Bernie Sanders authored proposed legislation entitled the Medicare For All Act of 2017. This proposal deserves special attention because it was cosponsored by seventeen senators, including Cory Booker, Kirsten Gillibrand, Kamala Harris, Jeff Merkley, and Elizabeth Warren—all of whom have either formally explored or declared their candidacy for the 2020 presidential election. What exactly did Senator Sanders author and the others cosponsor?

If Medicare were a private industry brand, then Senator Sanders and his Medicare for all proposal would be sued for copyright infringement or deceptive trade practices. Although I am confident it would not be popular at a campaign stop, the more appropriate name for the proposed plan is "Medicare for None" because it abolishes Medicare and virtually all of its existing structure and elements. In my mind, Medicare for all would mean that the existing Medicare program is the coverage that all Americans receive. Therefore, for clarity in this book, I will refer to Senator Sanders' proposal as Medicare for None.

How Does It Work?

- **Universal Coverage**—Everyone is covered by a single government program after a four-year phase-in.

- **No Out-of-Pocket Expense**—Eliminates all cost sharing when a person uses the healthcare system.

- **Provider Reimbursement**—Medicare reimbursement applies for all services.

- **Establishes the Agency for Healthcare Research and Quality.**

- **Prohibits the Sale of Private Insurance, Employer-Sponsored Insurance, and Individual Insurance** for services covered under the Universal Medicare Program. It is a single-payer system.

- **Abolishes Current Medicaid, CHIP, and Medicare** plans into the new Universal Medicare Program that covers everyone.

How Is It Funded?

Medicare for None exchanges premiums for taxes. Premiums for health insurance would no longer be required, but new taxes would be implemented to pay for the program. Although the proposed Medicare For All Act did not include a formal funding proposal, Senator Sanders released options for funding of the Medicare For All Act that provide an indication of required funding.

The following is a summary of how the act would be funded:

- a 7.5% employer-paid income tax;

- a 4% household income tax for households above $29,000 in income;

- $4.2 trillion in additional taxes from the elimination of employer-sponsored health insurance;

- tax increases for those with income greater than $250,000 (marginal rates would range from 40% up to 52% in the highest bracket);

- taxing capital gains at income-tax rates;

- cap all tax deductions at 28% for households at or above $250,000;

- more progressive and aggressive estate tax;

- establish a net-worth tax on the top .1%;

- eliminate the Gingrich-Edwards S-distribution loophole;

- impose a one-time tax on held offshore profits;

- impose a fee on large financial institutions; and/or

- repeal last-in, first-out (LIFO) accounting.

The ten-year cost estimates range from around $32 trillion to $37 trillion. At first glance, this seems like a staggering cost. It is, however, important to note that these cost estimates are less than the total projections for national health expenditures over ten years under the current system of public and private insurance. Medicare for None would cost substantially less in total than the current healthcare system. Negative comments from opponents who criticize the total cost either fail to recognize or choose to ignore that Senator Sanders' proposal is a net reduction in cost. The big financial difference is that all the funding is consolidated under federal government authority.

Medicare for All

Although Senator Kamala Harris is a cosponsor of Senator Sanders' proposed legislation, she has separated from him in her definition of Medicare for all. Senator Harris' Medicare For All Plan makes some changes to the current Medicare system but does allow private insurance as an alternative to the public program. It is very similar to current Medicare Advantage programs that provide a private alternative to traditional Medicare. The Harris Medicare For All Plan would transition all people into either the government Medicare plan or the Medicare private option over a ten-year period. Her plan allows anyone to opt in to the Medicare plan immediately if desired. (3)

Senator Harris supports many of Senator Sanders' funding ideas; however, she proposes that households earning below $100,000 per year be exempt from the new 4% income tax.

Although Senator Harris' plan is short on details, it does appear that it accomplishes many of the same goals of the Sanders' plan and could appropriately be called Medicare for all because it is based on the current Medicare program.

The Case for Medicare for None/All

The case for Medicare for none/all includes:

- **Medicare for all is the social-justice champion.** Ability to pay would never again be a factor in access to healthcare services in America. It solves the uninsured and all individual-affordability problems.

- **Medicare for all is simple.** Everyone is covered by the same public health insurance program, and it does not cost the individual anything when the individual accesses the healthcare system for services. It is significantly more administratively efficient. Medical providers do not have to have today's billing or collection services because they don't bill patients or insurance companies. Patients don't have to deal with medical bills. Healthcare is truly "free" for the patient at the time of service.

- **Medicare for all lowers healthcare costs.** I believe it is fair to say that Medicare for all saves money, even though it increases federal government expenditures. It simply concentrates all the money that is paid by the government, companies, and individuals for healthcare services into one government-controlled financing pool.

The social-justice, simplicity, and lower total cost wins will be appealing to many voters.

The Argument Against Medicare for None/All

The opponents of Medicare for all worry about the economy, healthcare access and innovation, and government overreach.

The Economy

Healthcare is not only the largest employer but also the greatest job creator in the country. Healthcare employs more people than any other industry in the US. (4) Over the past twenty years, three out of every ten net new private jobs were created in healthcare. (5) The Bureau of Labor statistics produced maps showing the industry with the highest employment by state from 1993 to 2013. The maps illustrate how we transitioned from a manufacturing country that made stuff in 1993, to a retail country that sold stuff in 2003, then to a healthcare country that tried to heal stuff by 2013.

As previously noted in this book, the average hospital loses 9.9% in treating Medicare patients because the cost to provide the care is higher than the Medicare reimbursement. (6) Private insurance pays hospitals 241% of the Medicare reimbursement rate. (7) This means private insurance pays a hospital $2.41 for the same services the hospital is willing to sell to Medicare for $1. Shifting all payments to Medicare reimbursement would create a massive reduction in healthcare funding and, potentially, a hole in the entire economy.

In a strange economic twist, the price discrimination and administrative inefficiency in healthcare *create* jobs. One person's cost growth is another person's new job. How many jobs could be eliminated through a lower-cost and more efficient healthcare system? I don't know, but I do know that a major reduction in the prices paid for healthcare services by those who are currently in the private insurance system would lead to a massive reduction in jobs in healthcare delivery, administration, and insurance. Direct healthcare jobs would not be the only jobs sacrificed. Healthcare construction would virtually cease with the elimination of profit in healthcare. Think about the building that used to house the Blockbuster video store in your neighborhood. There is reasonable likelihood it is now some type of health-related business. Healthcare has stepped in to fill retail space as digital services and online shopping have decreased the need for traditional retail bricks and mortar. Shrinking the healthcare economy would create a negative trickle-down impact to construction, real estate, and other industries.

Is this simply economic fearmongering? I hope not, and I don't think so. The healthcare industry relies on the profits from the private insurance reimbursement rates. Breaking the addiction to those private insurance reimbursement rates will not be without economic side effects.

An easy answer to the economic risk of lowering all reimbursements to the current Medicare level is to increase the Medicare reimbursements. Remember the solvency challenges that the Medicare Hospital Insurance trust fund faces? The fund is projected to become insolvent by 2026 under its current structure. Increasing the Medicare reimbursement rates would only accelerate and exacerbate the current Medicare financial struggles. The current Medicare program needs more revenue and *fewer* expenses to remain solvent.

Access and Innovation

Medicare reimbursement rates alone cannot financially support the healthcare access that Americans have come to expect. Any system based on Medicare reimbursement rates would dramatically lower the cost of private health insurance, but affordable health insurance without adequate access to healthcare services may not be an acceptable tradeoff for voters.

The net reduction in healthcare spending creates a concern for some regarding healthcare quality and innovation. Would a reduction in reimbursements in the US for healthcare services constrict private medical research, leading to a reduction in innovation? It is difficult to predict what would happen to medical research, but the profits from private reimbursements for research funding and as a research motivator would be gone.

Government Overreach

Some simply fear government overreach in healthcare. Would a lack of service competition lead to a health-insurance service equivalent of the IRS? Would the federal government be the sole authority on care decisions? What role would the federal government ultimately play in individual wellness? Would there be a government-determined rationing of care in an effort to balance future budgets? Opponents of Medicare for all believe that private industry provides an alternative and a balance to government authority.

Republicans, Libertarians, and conservatives aren't the only people to question Medicare for all's wisdom. Moderate Democrats also struggle to support the progressive Medicare-for-all approach. In addition to moderate Democrats, some key leaders like Nancy Pelosi see the ACA as part of their legacy and will look to protect and fix existing law rather than to replace it with a completely different system. Some view Medicare for all as an abandonment of the ACA. Essentially, Medicare for all is "repeal and replace" from the left, rather than from the right.

What's Next?

Americans have a generally favorable or generally negative view of the ACA based on their political affiliation rather than their intimate knowledge of the law. Medicare for all is following the same pattern of party-line approval and lack of real understanding. Republicans rallied around "repeal and replace" without knowing what the replacement might be. Medicare for all will be the rallying cry for Progressives even if there is great confusion as to what the phrase means.

Sources

(1) The Hill. "70 percent of Americans Prefer Medicare for All Proposal." Thehill.com. October 22, 2018.

(2) Yusra Murad. "Majority Backs 'Medicare for All' Replacing Private Plans, if Preferred Providers Stay." Morningconsult.com. July 2, 2019.

(3)   Kamala Harris. *My Plan For Medicare For All.* Medium.com. July 29, 2019.

(4)   Derek Thompson. "Health Care Just Became the U.S.'s Largest Employer." *The Atlantic.* January 9, 2018.

(5)   Federal Reserve Economic Data (FRED). "All Employees: Total Private Industries and Education and Health Services: Health Care. 1999-07-01 to 2019-07-01." Fred.stlouisfed.org.

(6)   MedPAC. "Report to the Congress: Medicare Payment Policy." Medpac.gov. March 15, 2019.

(7)   Chapin White and Christopher Whaley. "Prices Paid to Hospitals by Private Health Plans Are High Relative to Medicare and Vary Widely: Findings from an Employer-Led Transparency Initiative." Rand.org. May 9, 2019.

Chapter 16:

Medicare for More, Medicaid Light, and Other Public-Plan Options

THE ACA EXTENDED HEALTH INSURANCE coverage to approximately twenty million people, but more than twenty-seven million Americans still have no health insurance protection. Those who receive their health insurance through private sources still see healthcare inflation that is outpacing growth in GDP and growth in wages. Those in Washington, DC, who want to fix the ACA need to answer this key question: Is there a way to cover more people for less money and to lower the cost for everyone? An answer of *yes* to this question would mean we fixed the ACA. So, what are the proposals to do it?

Democratic Proposals

Republicans are on their heels after their repeal-and-replace failures. The debate regarding healthcare options will be driven by Democratic candidates. While Progressive Democrats support Medicare for all, the more moderate Democrat proposals include less-disruptive solutions that attempt to better connect public and private insurance programs to help fix the ACA's ills. The main variances in the proposals relate to the program platform and eligibility.

- **Platform**—Medicare, Medicaid, or a new public-plan option could create additional choice and competition in health insurance. Some proposals create a new federal program that would compete with private insurance. The new public option would be available through the Marketplace. Other options skip the creation of a new program and simply allow people to enroll in the existing Medicare or Medicaid programs.

- **Eligibility**—Public programs could be available to anyone as an alternative to private insurance. Eligibility could be limited to only those who are not eligible for employer-sponsored coverage. Eligibility could have an age or income threshold. The range of eligibility options is broad.

- **Age-Based Buy-In**—One option is to allow individuals to buy in to Medicare at an earlier age, like fifty or fifty-five. This approach could provide a lower-cost option for those who are at the most expensive levels of the individual health insurance rate table. The irony of lowering Medicare's eligibility age is that Social Security eligibility has already been raised to age sixty-seven from age sixty-five in order to lower the government's cost of the program. The CBO has provided Congress with a cost estimate of increasing Medicare eligibility to age sixty-seven to align with Social Security. The Social Security change and the CBO cost estimates conflict with the age-based Medicare buy-in concept.

- **Marketplace Option**—This approach would put the Medicare, Medicaid, or public option on the Marketplace for individual health insurance only. Individuals eligible for affordable employer-sponsored health insurance coverage would not be eligible for a subsidized public-plan option. Limiting the public option to only the individual marketplace would be a more palatable solution for pharmaceutical and hospital lobby groups because it would keep the more lucrative private insurance reimbursement in place for employer-sponsored health plans. This approach could result in further cost shifting making employer-sponsored insurance even more expensive.

- **Marketplace Plus Small-Employer Option**—The offer rate of health insurance for small employers is much lower than for large employers. One option is to open the public plan to small employers to encourage more employment-based health insurance coverage through a lower-cost public option.

- **Medicare for All Who Want It**—At least one Democratic proposal would open a newly developed Medicare program— Medicare Part E—as an option for all employers to offer for their employer-sponsored health plan. Most other proposals keep large employers out of the public-plan option.

Americans are not highly satisfied with the current state of healthcare options. Politicians are busy crafting potential new health insurance options to woo voters.

Public-Plan Option

The original House and Senate bills that ultimately led to the ACA included the creation of a public-plan option that would have been offered on the Exchange alongside the insurance company plan options. The public plan would have been government-run and would have based its reimbursements to providers on Medicare payment structures. One approach proposed paying medical providers the Medicare rate plus 5%, and the other proposed paying Medicare plus 10%. This reimbursement level is far less than what the private insurance market pays.

In the end, these public-plan options were negotiated out of the final ACA legislation. Resistance to the public-plan option came from both hospital and insurance-company interest groups. It would have been difficult for private insurance companies to compete with a plan that paid medical providers substantially less for medical services. The insurance industry would either be eliminated by the lower-cost public-plan competition or demand significantly lower rates that are closer to the public-plan levels from medical providers. Under either competitive scenario, I believe a public-plan option would have lowered the cost of health insurance because it would have reduced the amount paid to medical providers.

Instead of a public-plan option, the ACA created co-ops to compete with private insurance. The co-ops were not-for-profit insurance entities created with federal subsidies to try to create competition for insurance companies and choice for consumers. Nineteen of the twenty-three co-ops created have failed and are no longer operating. (1) There are a host of reasons for the failures, but the bottom line is that most underpriced the health insurance risk and were relying on government subsidies for financial sustainability.

I was giving a speech in Wisconsin soon after the first co-ops failed. I explained to the group how the government-created and -subsidized co-ops were intentionally underpricing health insurance to gain market share and that the government's unwillingness to provide unlimited funds was causing failures. A gentleman in the back of the room stood up and let me know he was an actuary who had worked for several of the now-failing co-ops. He explained that the co-ops had been founded to create competition and had not been intended to make money or break even. His view was that the government broke its promise by limiting its financial subsidies to cover the co-op losses. My view was that taxpayer money was squandered by a bad idea. Health insurance is expensive because healthcare is expensive, and the co-ops did nothing to lower the cost of care; they simply used taxpayer money to underprice their competition.

The failure of the ACA-created co-op program decreases my confidence in the government's ability to create a new program to compete with private insurance. Price manipulation and government-subsidy reliance are not effective building blocks for a sustainable, successful business. Therefore, the utilization of either Medicare or Medicaid as a public-plan option, rather than the creation of a new entity or program, inspires greater confidence.

Medicaid Light

What if the Health Insurance Marketplace, formerly called the Exchange, had been called Medicaid Light? It might have been a more appropriate moniker. Medicaid is the taxpayer-funded health insurance program for low-income participants. The Marketplace is the predominantly taxpayer-funded health insurance program for individuals who make up to 400% of the FPL and do not have access to affordable health insurance through an employer. The average annual Marketplace subsidy per enrollee increased to $6,696 in 2018 from $3,108 in 2014. (2) The average subsidy is 86% of the total premium. (3) With this percentage of taxpayer funding, it is fair to categorize the subsidized Marketplace as a public program. Is it an efficient use of taxpayer dollars to reimburse providers at private insurance network reimbursement rates for a publicly funded program?

Pop Quiz

Please select the answer that best describes your belief.

A. The Health Insurance Marketplace is a public program funded primarily by taxpayers and should reimburse medical providers at public-program levels.

B. Although the Health Insurance Marketplace is primarily taxpayer-funded, it is built on the private insurance system. Therefore, it is appropriate to pay medical providers at private-insurance levels.

If your answer is "A," then you might unknowingly be a supporter of Medicaid Light.

How would Medicaid Light differ from the Marketplace that was created or from a public-plan option that was considered? Medicaid Light could use the Medicaid administration-and-reimbursement platform. Medicaid has experienced the lowest rate of inflation among health-plan types over the past decade, while the individual insurance market has experienced the highest rate of inflation. (4) Medicaid reimburses medical providers far less than private insurance does. I believe Medicaid Light would have produced a financially and administratively less burdensome approach to subsidized health insurance.

Medicaid Light could also be a platform for a public-plan option. If the federal government, or even a state government, decides that a public plan needs to be offered as competition for private insurance in the Marketplace, Medicaid is an existing program that could be offered. Utilizing existing Medicaid for a public-plan option, rather than creating a new program, would increase speed to market and decrease administrative costs.

Calling the Obamacare Marketplace "Medicaid Light" would have significant public-perception challenges. People want an "Advanceable Premium Tax Credit" (the official name of the healthcare subsidy) to lower their cost of healthcare premiums. The Medicaid Light naming would not change the subsidy system, but it potentially carries the sense of being a government handout if "Medicaid" is in the name. The subsidy could be interpreted as a premium offset if used to purchase private insurance through the Marketplace, or the same subsidy could be viewed as a government handout if referred to as Medicaid Light. On average, Medicare participants pay approximately 14% of the total premium. This is almost identical to the percentage of premium paid on average within the subsidized Marketplace. I don't believe people consider Medicare a "government handout," but I sense that leveraging the Medicaid platform and naming could be viewed negatively by subsidized participants. The name matters!

Medicare for More

Multiple Democratic proposals include expanded Medicare eligibility. Mayor Pete Buttigieg refers to his approach as Medicare for All Who Want It. I call it Medicare for more. Unlike Medicare for all, Medicare for more would use the existing Medicare program but would expand eligibility.

The Medicare for more options surround eligibility and cost. The first question about Medicare expansion is who would be newly eligible. Some proposals lower the Medicare eligibility to age fifty-five, and others would make all ages eligible. Some proposals would provide Medicare as an option only for individual Marketplace participants; others would include small employers; and some would open Medicare as an option for all individuals and groups.

The second question is how much they would pay. Existing Medicare premium rates are indexed based on income but do not have any age variance. As previously mentioned, taxpayers fund approximately 86% of the cost of Medicare, and participants pay about 14% on average. How would Medicare funding rates be set for newly eligible populations, and how much of the premium would they pay?

The Case for Medicare for More

Medicare is a popular and effective public-private partnership. The cost for Medicare would be lower than the cost of private health insurance because Medicare pays medical providers less than private insurance does. Expanding the existing Medicare program is infinitely easier than creating a new program. It lowers cost and is easy to implement . . . what's not to love?

The Argument Against Medicare for More

Expanding Medicare eligibility seems like a low-risk, easy fix to some of the current Marketplace problems. Medicare has one potential financial hurdle, however: The Medicare Hospital Insurance trust fund is on a path to insolvency by 2026 because expenses are projected to be larger than revenues in Medicare each year until then. Any expansion of Medicare would need to enhance Medicare's solvency through excess premiums and not further threaten its solvency. Expanding eligibility without fully funding the newly covered population could further jeopardize Medicare's financial future. The federal government's history of underfunding entitlement expansions gives me little confidence that Medicare for more would carry its own financial weight.

Medicare enrollment is growing even with no change in eligibility rules because of the aging demographic mix in America. Politicians are talking about potentially adding a substantial number of people into Medicare through their eligibility-expansion plans. The final chapter of the opening section of the 2019 Medicare Trustees report summarizes Medicare's current financial position:

> The financial projections in this report indicate a need for substantial changes to address Medicare's financial challenges. The sooner solutions are enacted, the more flexible and gradual they can be. The early introduction of reforms increases the time available for affected individuals and organizations—including health care providers, beneficiaries, and taxpayers—to adjust their expectations and behavior. The Trustees recommend that Congress and the executive branch work closely together with a sense of urgency to address these challenges. (5)

Do you believe Congress and the executive branch are working closely together with a sense of urgency to address Medicare's financial challenges? The campaign discussions involving Medicare fail to mention Medicare's tenuous financial position. The Medicare Trustees are telling Congress and the president to get to work solving Medicare's financial struggle and to do it now. They are telling healthcare providers, beneficiaries, and taxpayers to get ready for potentially significant changes. Benefits or eligibility might get limited, premiums might increase, payments to medical providers might drop, and taxes might need to increase. Status quo in Medicare financing is a financial dead-end road. Adding new groups of people into Medicare without honestly confronting the financial challenges is like moving people on to the coastline with an active hurricane warning. The Medicare Trustees are sounding the economic warning siren, but politicians are talking about inward migration rather than an evacuation plan.

So, why aren't politicians talking about Medicare's financing challenges, and why aren't legislators doing anything about it? Medicare is popular. Raising taxes, cutting benefits, and cutting payments to medical providers is not! Therefore, candidates enthusiastically discuss expanding Medicare rather than publicly discuss the program's challenging financial future.

Could Medicare expansion help solve the perilous financial outlook? Yes, if the revenue generated from the newly eligible populations is greater than the cost to provide the benefits—in other words, if the program is profitable. The federal government's track record of responsibly funding entitlement programs is poor and contributes to our debt and annual deficit problems. Expanding the Medicare promise is a great way to get votes, but adequately funding Medicare's rising cost is not.

Expect pharmaceutical and hospital industry groups to vehemently oppose Medicare expansion. Groups like the Partnership for America's Health Care Future (PAHCF) are aligning stakeholders against expansion of public programs. Logos on the PAHCF website include America's Health Insurance Plans, American Hospital Association, Blue Cross Blue Shield Association, National Association of Health Underwriters, PhRMA, and many others. What could possibly bring these traditional adversaries together? Medicare expansion means lost revenue for many stakeholders, and the loss of money can bring traditional adversaries together to fight a common enemy. Expect the ads from groups like PAHCF to send a message of lack of choice, lack of access, and lack of innovation in healthcare.

What's Next?

A public-plan option is a logical compromise that sits between the status quo and Medicare for all. Expect moderate Democrats to embrace this approach as a way to fix Obamacare by expanding choice and lowering cost through new competition. The real question for moderate Democrats is which program and expanded to whom?

Sources

(1) National Association of Insurance Commissioners. "Health Insurance Cooperative." Naic.org. April 18, 2019.

(2) ASPE Research Brief. "2019 Health Plan Choice and Premiums in Healthcare.gov States." Aspe.hhs.gov. October 26, 2018.

(3) Centers for Medicare and Medicaid Services. "Health Insurance Exchanges 2018 Open Enrollment Period Final Report." Cms.gov. April 3, 2018.

(4) Centers for Medicare and Medicaid Services. "National Health Expenditure Data, National Health Expenditures by Type of Service and Source of Fund, CY 1960–2017." Cms.gov. April 17, 2018.

(5) Centers for Medicare and Medicaid Services. "2019 Annual Report of the Boards of Trustees of the Federal Hospital Insurance and Federal Supplementary Medical Insurance Trust Funds." Cms.gov. April 22, 2019.

Chapter 17:

All-Payer System
and Medicare Indexing

REMEMBER THE GLORY DAYS OF Bill Clinton's first term in office? Many Millennial voters were not born yet, and many of them who were already born were far more interested in the Disney Channel and Nickelodeon than CNN or Fox News. President Clinton had put his wife, Hillary Clinton, in charge of a group evaluating healthcare options for America. The result of the analysis was called the Health Security Act of 1993, or HillaryCare. Preferred provider organization networks, also known as PPOs, were a child of the late 1980s. Insurance companies were negotiating discounts with hospitals and doctors. These PPO networks were paying hospitals more than Medicare for the same services. The HillaryCare plan had a solution: What if everyone paid the same as Medicare for hospital and other medical provider services? This concept is known as an all-payer plan, which allows public and private healthcare systems to coexist, with the price of healthcare services determined by a government, or government-authorized, entity.

The following starts the prologue in an article in *Health Affairs*: "The endless debate over the future shape of our healthcare financing system has focused on the continuum between market competition and government regulation and the question: Which is right for Americans?" The article itself begins, "As health care costs continue to soar, interest in cost containment has reached a new height. Extreme pressure on federal and state government spending and stress on private purchasers from the recession and international competition have intensified payers' efforts to restrain increases in outlays for health care." (1)

This article was addressing the question of how market competition and government regulation should connect because rising healthcare costs were intensifying economic pressure from a recent recession and increasing global competition. No, this article did not appear in *Health Affairs* last year. This article was published in the summer of 1992. The issues that our country faced in the early 1990s regarding healthcare, the economy, government, and the private sector look eerily similar to the issues we face as we enter the 2020s. It was this environment in which Hillary Clinton's committee evaluated connecting public and private medical-service payment rates. The gap between private and private-payer reimbursement rates has multiplied, and the link between public- and private-payer reimbursement rates is once again being considered in Washington, DC.

The CBO analyzed over 600,000 hospital stays incurred in 2013 to determine how commercial insurance reimbursements compared to Medicare. After adjusting for condition, location, and severity, the CBO found that commercial insurers paid approximately 90% more than Medicare for identical hospital stays in 2013. (2) The gap has widened since this study. The Rand Corporation studied hospital prices in twenty-five states in 2017 and found that privately insured patients paid 241% of what Medicare would have paid for the same procedures. (3) Studies may find different price-discrimination results based on the timing and data utilized, but the gap is real, and the gap is widening.

An all-payer system eliminates price discrimination by allowing all payers to reimburse at a single government-determined price for a given service at a given medical provider.

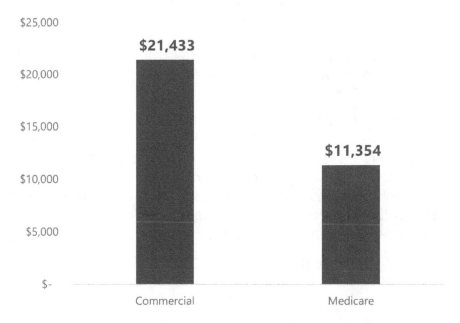

PRICE PER STAY

Source: Congressional Budget Office. "An Analysis of Private-Sector Prices for Hospital Admissions: Working Paper 2017–02." Cbo.gov. April 4, 2017.

The Case for All-Payer

An all-payer system would eliminate price discrimination. Simplicity and competition could enter the health insurance marketplace. Health insurance costs would drop substantially for the majority of Americans who are insured through their employers or through individually purchased insurance. The insurance and patient savings would be real, immediate, and sustainable. Price inflation could be controlled through the centralized government negotiating health prices. Hospitals and insurance companies could compete for business based on transparent cost and service quality on a level playing field. Network discount-negotiating strength would no longer be a barrier to entry for health insurance, leading to new insurance competitors and choices for consumers.

A campaign speech in favor of an all-payer system might start with something like this: "My plan allows you to keep the insurance you have today and to receive medical services at the hospital you choose. The big difference is that you will pay what the government pays for services. The insurance companies are colluding to discriminate against you today. That is why health insurance is so expense. I will outlaw this abusive practice and lower the cost of insurance for the average American family by over $10,000 per year. What will *you* do with your $10,000?"

This has all the elements of a perfect campaign pitch. There's a villain—actually, two; the hospitals and insurance companies are easy targets. There's a victim—that's you, but it's not your fault. There's a sniveling sheriff who is incapable of saving anyone—that's the current politician who allowed this mess. And there's a hero—that's the candidate giving the speech, of course. Vote for the hero. You get all the benefits, and there's no cost and no tax increase.

It sounds like all-payer is the perfect political and economic solution, but is it?

The Argument Against All-Payer

The same economic, healthcare-access, and innovation concerns of the Medicare-for-all approach apply to the all-payer approach. The healthcare economy bubble is propped up by the opaque discriminatory pricing mechanisms that fuel the high cost of private health insurance. The system is a job creator, construction stimulant, and care-innovation funder. An all-payer system would remove 100% of the profit from an industry that has been one of America's great job creators as well as real estate developers and the world's health-cure researcher.

A dramatic decrease in private-payer reimbursement rates would lead to massive job losses in healthcare. Investment dollars for medical research would shrink. Healthcare-related construction would cease. The retail real estate market has already been impacted by online shopping and digital services. Healthcare services have absorbed some of the retail space that was once occupied by companies like Blockbuster video; many of these retail healthcare outposts would be abandoned as healthcare facilities contracted into their hospital hubs.

ALL-PAYER EARTHQUAKE

Put simply, I believe a pure all-payer system would pop the healthcare economic bubble and plunge the US into a second Great Depression. Sure, it's an ominous opinion, but the job loss, real estate, and construction crises that would follow would be like combining an economic hurricane, tidal wave, and earthquake.

Is There a Compromise Solution?

Yes! Elements of all-payer make great sense and could substantially lower the cost of health insurance premiums, simplify the health consumer experience for patients and providers, and improve competition. Instead of popping the healthcare economic balloon, think about using elements of all-payer to intentionally let air out of the balloon over time through an organized and systematic linking of healthcare prices to what the government pays. Rather than mirroring government prices, which I believe would crash the healthcare economic system, all other payers could cap what they pay as a percentage of what the government pays, on a decreasing scale over ten to fifteen years. Hospitals could adjust their business practices and investments to maintain profitability and financial viability in a "new normal." The decreasing scale could effectively eliminate most health insurance inflation for a decade or more.

North Carolina's Clear Pricing Plan was a state-based attempt to index provider payments to Medicare. Reference-based pricing is a market-driven attempt to mirror this type of Medicare indexing. These reference-based programs cap what insurance pays as a percentage of what Medicare pays. In other words, they *index* their pricing to Medicare as a benchmark. Although relatively new, these programs are creating a stir in the insurance marketplace but are receiving strong resistance from hospitals in some geographic markets. Public-program payment systems, like Medicare, create either a cost-shifting wave that other payers must fight against or a pathway that others can follow.

The State of Washington has introduced Cascade Care, scheduled to be effective in January 2021, for people purchasing health insurance in the individual market. Cascade Care is a state-run public-private partnership. The state regulates the consumer premium cost share and out-of-pocket expenses. It also regulates reimbursements to medical providers by capping the maximum reimbursement at 160% of the Medicare reimbursement rate. The program will be administered by existing private health insurance companies so the state does not have to establish or maintain an insurance-administration entity.

Another form of indexing is a balance-billing limit. Medicare has a balance-billing limit for physician services that protects Medicare consumers by capping the legal billing amount a physician can charge. The ACA put caps on insurance company loss ratios, but it did nothing to protect consumers against discriminatory pricing schemes. The result has been a widening gap between what Medicare pays for services and what individuals covered by private insurance pay for the same services. A balance-billing limit linked to Medicare reimbursement schedules could provide consumer protection by filling a void left open by the ACA. A Medicare index could be the missing link that allows healthcare financing to successfully evolve.

The Case for Medicare Indexing

Medicare indexing creates a platform that proactively connects public and private medical reimbursements. It recognizes the economic and quality-of-care risks of an all-payer system and the economic risks of the status quo. It provides a pathway to methodically reduce the payment-discrimination gap over time without dramatically reducing access to high-quality healthcare. It would also lower the cost of health insurance, stabilize the private insurance market, and increase competition among insurance companies.

The Argument Against Medicare Indexing

One needs to look no further than North Carolina to see the resistance that hospitals have to Medicare indexing. The major hospitals there vehemently resisted the state's attempt to link reimbursements to Medicare even if the reimbursements approached two times what

Medicare pays. The argument made by the hospitals was that Medicare indexing would reduce access to care and quality of care. The political argument against Medicare indexing is that it is government overreach and creates a form of government price controls or price fixing.

Medicare indexing is a form of government price fixing, but what if the prices need to be fixed? If care were affordable, if every American had health insurance protection, and if healthcare expenses did not create personal bankruptcy for so many American families, then protection of status-quo pricing might be justifiable. But I believe healthcare pricing is broken and needs to be fixed! I believe voters who understand how the system really works, or doesn't work, would agree.

What's Next?

The status-quo protection forces of the current private insurance system are resisting transformative pricing. Those on the far left may see transformative pricing as an inadequate step toward the goal of a single-payer system, and those on the far right may resist it as intrusive government price controls. It is politically difficult to answer why unbridled price discrimination in healthcare is legal. State initiatives, like Washington state's Cascade Care, could open the door to a national debate on all-payer or Medicare indexing.

Sources

(1)   Paul Ginsburg and Kenneth Thorpe. "Can All-Payer Rate Setting and the Competitive Strategy Coexist?" Healthaffairs.org. Summer 1992.

(2)   Congressional Budget Office. "An Analysis of Private-Sector Prices for Hospital Admissions: Working Paper 2017–02." Cbo.gov. April 4, 2017.

(3)   Chapin White and Christopher Whaley. "Prices Paid to Hospitals by Private Health Plans Are High Relative to Medicare and Vary Widely: Findings from an Employer-Led Transparency Initiative." Rand.org. 2019.

Chapter 18:

Is the Employer Exit Door Open?

EMPLOYER-SUBSIDIZED COVERAGE IS THE largest source of coverage for Americans under age sixty-five, covering 159 million people. Keeping employer money in the healthcare equation is vitally important.

SOURCE OF HEALTH INSURANCE FOR PEOPLE UNDER AGE 65

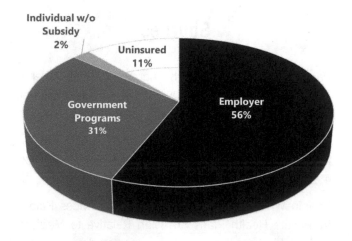

Source: Congressional Budget Office. "Federal Subsidies for Health Insurance Coverage for People Under Age 65." Cbo.gov. May 2, 2019.

A key reason for the large-employer mandate in the ACA was keeping employers and their money in the game. An exit by employers would put unbearable pressure on the federal budget, deficits, and debt, meaning that the employer money would have to be replaced through massive new taxes.

Health insurance is financially and administratively expensive. Wellness- and disease-management interventions have been added to employer plans to control cost, but the financial return is questionable, and these programs can also become culturally expensive. Employees and their family members can become frustrated with these insurance requirements and restrictions. So, why do employers stay in the health insurance business?

- First, the tax preference for employer-sponsored health insurance makes it a good value for the company and employees, despite the high price tag.

- Second, at 4% unemployment, there is a war for talent. A good health-benefit plan is a strong retention tool when an employee starts to look at the real cost and options for health insurance on the individual market.

- Third, the large employer mandate creates a stay incentive for employers with fifty or more full-time employees.

Employers have found themselves reluctant providers of the most costly, most complicated, and worst-performing healthcare system in the economically developed world. It is hard for them to feel great about this investment.

Employer-sponsored retirement plans were once dominated by pension plans, where the employer guaranteed a post-retirement income stream to former employees. Employers accepted the investment risk for the guaranteed payment plans. These defined-benefit plans have given way to defined-contribution 401(k) plans. The employer accepts no investment risk in the 401(k) plan; they will provide enrollment, communication, administration, and financial support, but the investment risk is on the plan participant. The dream of flipping employer-sponsored health insurance to a defined-contribution approach like a 401(k) is not new. It started with "cafeteria" plans, which allowed employees to choose among benefit plan options. The problem with the cafeteria-plan approach is that the employer is still the underwriting unit for healthcare pricing and the "community" for determining rates is employees and their covered family members. Therefore, risk still sits at an employer level, and higher claims means higher costs for the company and its employees.

The hope reemerged when the ACA created the Health Insurance Marketplace, then known as the Exchange. The Exchange created a market where subsidized individuals could apply a government-provided tax credit to purchase any insurance plan from any insurance company on the Exchange. Insurance consultants quickly moved to create private exchanges that would mirror the government model. Business consultants predicted a market takeover in the employer-sponsored space by these newly created private exchanges. A 2013 headline infamously proclaimed, "One-in-Four Consumers Will Receive Employer Health Benefits Through Insurance Exchanges in Five Years, Accenture Research Shows." (1) Finally, employers could stop choosing a health plan for their employees and could give them the money to make their own choices through the newly created private exchanges. Employer-facilitated, rather than employer-centric, health insurance would soon dominate the market. At least, that was the forecast.

Although private exchanges still exist, their market penetration has been minimal. The original private-exchange vision has not come to fruition for a very basic reason: The individual employer group is still the underwriting unit in employer-sponsored health insurance. The cost of insurance for a company's employees is based on the claims history, risk factors, and known conditions for its unique employee-and-family group. To keep things affordable, employers still needed to positively influence risk, and the private-exchange platform was in direct opposition to this risk-influence need.

The ACA eliminated all medical underwriting so all employees and family members could purchase individual coverage through the Marketplace with no risk of preexisting-condition limitations. If an employer wanted to use the individual Marketplace rather than their group insurance plan as the insurance coverage for their employees, then they would lose the tax-preferred status of employer-sponsored health insurance for both company and employee dollars. As an employer, you either maintained your group as a risk unit or you forfeited the tax benefits. In addition, in this scenario, large employers would be subject to the ACA penalty for not offering a plan. Paying for health insurance on a posttax basis and paying a penalty for not offering a plan was no real option at all. In the end, employers realized they could not abdicate their risk- and cost-influence responsibilities.

President Obama Cracks Open the Window

Enter the 21st Century Cures Act, which was signed into law in December 2016 as one of President Obama's legislative actions. This quiet piece of legislation was a massive opportunity for small businesses, creating qualified small-employer health-reimbursement arrangements (QSERHRAs). A QSERHRA allows a small employer— defined as an employer having fewer than fifty full-time employees— to put money into an account that employees can use to get a tax-free reimbursement for purchasing healthcare services, including health insurance. Employees can purchase coverage in the Marketplace or through a spouse's plan, a sharing ministry program, or any other platform. In 2019, the cap on employer deposits was $5,150 for single coverage and $10,450 for family. Employers that offer a group health, dental, or vision plan are not eligible to use a QSERHRA. In other words, QSERHRA is not an option that can be offered alongside employer coverage; it is all or none.

With QSERHRA, a small employer can truly move to a defined-contribution health-benefit program using pretax dollars. The risk and claims of individuals who work for the employer have no impact at all on the cost of insurance. The individual health insurance market is age-rated and heavily regulated post-ACA. Most CEOs and CFOs of large organizations have never heard of QSERHRA, and they might be very frustrated if they had. This product is much closer to the original private-exchange vision that Accenture predicted would move the entire market, but it is limited to small employers only.

President Trump Unlocks the Door

QSERHRA created an opportunity for small employers who were not subject to the ACA mandate, but large employers had no relief. Enter Executive Order 13813. In 2017, President Trump issued this executive order referred to as "Promoting Healthcare Choice and Competition Across the United States." It sounds a bit like "make healthcare great again," but I think he had already used that slogan. The executive order directed the secretaries of treasury, labor, and health and human services (HHS) to explore the use of health-reimbursement arrangements (HRAs) to be used in conjunction with nongroup coverage. The new program created by the executive order is known as an individual coverage health-reimbursement arrangement (ICHRA). An ICHRA allows an employer to put pretax money into an account for employees, who can then purchase an individual health insurance plan. An employee can purchase a plan through the Health Insurance Marketplace or can select an "off Exchange" individual plan. In either case, they can use the ICHRA money to reimburse for premiums and out-of-pocket expenses. An employer can even set up a system to capture the employee's share of premium on a pretax basis so both the employer and employee premium payments are pretax, just like in an employer-sponsored plan. (2)

ICHRA creates an unprecedented opportunity for employers of any size to evolve health insurance to a defined-contribution approach in the same way they moved from pension plans to defined-contribution (401(k)) plans. Employers can truly move to employer-facilitated plans with defined contributions and get away from the risk, wellness, renewal, and administrative tasks associated with today's employer-sponsored plans.

The Case for ICHRA

ICHRA holds great promise for employer relief from the administration and risk associated with employer-sponsored health insurance. Insurance companies will likely embrace the market opportunity. Hospitals, physicians, and the pharmaceutical industry will like the fact that ICHRA is built on private insurance rather than on a public plan. Employees may like the flexibility of changing jobs and not having to change insurance plans because of the job change. Republicans like it because it promotes consumerism. Democrats like it because it separates health insurance from employment and also potentially strengthens the individual Marketplace, providing long-term stability for Obamacare.

The Argument Against ICHRA

A few market factors will likely slow the flood to these ICHRA programs:

- **Newness**—Human Resource executives may be hesitant to abandon traditional health insurance in the current tight labor market. Administration companies are scrambling to build systems and programs to support ICHRA. Agents, brokers, and consultants must educate their customers.

- **Unfamiliar Choices**—Employers lack familiarity with individual plan offerings and operations. Companies like Molina and Oscar operate in the individual market but are unknown to employer-plan sponsors.

- **Limited Choices**—The options available in the individual marketplace are not as robust as the options in the employer-sponsored space in most parts of the country. Employers will have to be comfortable with the limited choices available to employees in some geographies or wait for choice to grow over time.

Progressives may argue that for-profit health insurance companies, for-profit pharmaceutical companies, and for-profit hospitals cannot be trusted in a private health insurance platform and that the ICHRA fails to solve any real issues because of the underlying profit motives of stakeholders.

Will ICHRA Become the 401(k) of Health Insurance?

In a game of dominoes, every domino played has an impact on the next domino to be played. The options you have when it is your turn to play are determined by the plays that have already occurred. Healthcare resembles a game of dominoes in that every change creates or closes opportunities. The ICHRA domino has already been played. It is available and requires no further legislative or regulatory action. There is a series of events that could create a path through which ICHRA plans could sweep the country in a matter of a few years. Follow this potential game of healthcare dominoes.

1. **Medicare for All Does Not Happen**—A Medicare-for-all program would wipe out the need for ICHRA. For my scenario, let's assume Medicare for all stretches the country's thoughts around the role of public and private insurance systems, but it is not implemented. The Medicare-for-all dialogue moves the fences.

2. **Medicare for More Happens**—Medicare for more becomes a reality. Concern over cost and choice in the individual health insurance market allows the federal government to offer Medicare plans as an option in the Marketplace to lower cost and increase choice. The lower Medicare cost means a reduction in the Obamacare bill for taxpayers because the required subsidies would be less expensive.

3. **Medicare For More . . . but Not You**—Medicare for more does not include employer-sponsored health insurance. Concern over decreased revenues for hospitals and pharmaceutical

companies in Medicare-based programs means the industries are able to restrict the expansion to the individual insurance market. Employers are restricted to traditional network approaches. In essence, for employers, it becomes Medicare for More but Not for You. The largest group of health insurance participants is still not eligible for Medicare in this scenario. Private insurance reimbursements grow to exceed 300% of Medicare as hospitals shift additional cost to employer plans while lower-revenue Medicare enrollment grows.

4. **Employers and Employees Want Relief**—Employers and employees remain frustrated by continued health insurance rate increases. The value of individually purchased Medicare plans is so much better than the employer-sponsored traditional products (thanks to the provider-reimbursement differential) that employers and employees gladly exchange their traditional coverage for ICHRA-facilitated Medicare options purchased in the individual market. The individual market provides better value and choice for employers and employees.

5. **Noah, Get Your Boat Ready!**—There is a market flood of enrollment in individual health insurance as employers abandon traditional employer-sponsored coverage. The massive increase in individual plan enrollment permanently stabilizes the individual health insurance market. The Obamacare Marketplace is ultimately fixed by Trump's executive order.

6. **Peace in Washington, DC**—In a health insurance act of God, both Democrats and Republicans are satisfied. Democrats realize Obamacare is fixed. Republicans realize employers are out of health insurance and that consumers can now make insurance choices.

Will the dominoes fall this way? I don't know. My crystal ball on healthcare is pretty good, but I am no Nostradamus when it comes to predicting politics; I thought Ivanka had a better chance than Donald at becoming president of the US. If the right political dominoes are played, the little-known ICHRA could become the key that unlocks the future of healthcare in America.

What's Next?

The expansion of the QSERHRA to the large-employer space via ICHRA is a potential marketplace earthquake. It could give large employers the opportunity to truly move into defined-contribution healthcare programs. Medicare for more, all-payer, or Medicare indexing could combine with ICHRA to totally reinvent the employer health insurance industry. Stay tuned on this one!

Sources

(1) Accenture. "One-in-Four Consumers Will Receive Employer Health Benefits Through Insurance Exchanges in Five Years, Accenture Research Shows." Accenture.com. June 3, 2013.

(2) *Federal Register*. "Health Reimbursement Arrangement and Other Account-Based Group Health Plans." Federalregister.gov. June 20, 2019.

Chapter 19:

Canada for All

OUR NEIGHBOR CANADA IS OFTEN used as a comparator for what the US healthcare system could be. One hundred percent (100%) of Canadians are covered through their publicly funded healthcare program; average Canadian life expectancy is longer than for their southern neighbors; and Canada spends less than half of what the US spends per person on healthcare. Universal coverage, longer life, and half the cost? Sing it with me: "Oh, Canada!" Who wouldn't sign up for this? We will call this approach Canada for All.

These facts are correct, but they don't tell the whole story of what Canada has and how its healthcare system differs from that of the US.

What Is the Canadian Healthcare System?

The Canadian healthcare system provides universal coverage based on need rather than on the ability to pay. (1) The system is based on shared funding and shared responsibility between provinces, territories, and the federal government.

The 1984 Canada Health Act (CHA) is Canada's federal legislation for publicly funded health insurance. It outlines five principles for the Canadian healthcare system:

- **Public Administration**—The government, whether provincial, territorial, or federal, is ultimately responsible for the administration of the health funding system.

- **Comprehensive**—All medically necessary services are covered.

- **Universality**—All Canadians are covered on uniform terms and conditions.

- **Accessibility**—Medical care and services must be reasonably accessible, without barriers.

- **Portability**—Care must be available as people move within Canada or travel abroad.

There is plan coverage variability by province, and there is no nationally established uniform plan design. For covered services, there is no cost-sharing for physician, diagnostic, or hospital services. Supplemental coverage provided by the public plan may include outpatient pharmacy, nonphysician mental health, vision, dental, home health, and hospice services, but coverage for these supplemental items varies by province. The government plan does not cover all expenses for all services. Total consumer out-of-pocket exposure under CHA is approximately 14% of the nation's total health spending. Private insurers cannot duplicate publicly covered items, but supplemental coverage is very common to reimburse for out-of-pocket expenses not covered under the public plan. A higher percentage of Canadians than Americans has private insurance. The primary difference is that Canadian private plans *supplement* government coverage, whereas most American private insurance is the *only* source of coverage for the participant. The Canadian system discourages the practice of extra billing; therefore, to avoid price discrimination, the government reimbursement level is the standard for all services. (2)

How Do Costs Compare?

Canada's total healthcare spending per capita is less than half that of the US.

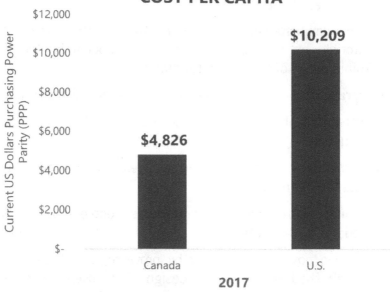

TOTAL ANNUAL HEALTHCARE COST PER CAPITA

Source: Organisation for Economic Co-operation and Development. "OECD Health Statistics." OECD Health Data. 2018.

The fact that Canada spends less per capita than the US is likely not a big surprise to most readers. What may be surprising is that the US spends more per capita on government-provided healthcare programs than Canada does, even though the American public system covers only 36% of the population. The Organisation for Economic Co-operation and Development (OECD) changed its categorization of the US system beginning in 2014 with the implementation of the ACA. Therefore, 2013 is the last credible year to use OECD data to compare the US and Canada for public insurance programs. In 2013, the US surprisingly spent 34% *more* per capita for government healthcare programs than Canada did, while covering only 36% of the population. Canada spent less and covered everyone. The naïve assumption that the US could lower its healthcare cost to something like that of Canada by simply shifting the entire population to a public insurance program, like Medicare, is proven dramatically false by this problematic cost truth. We already spend more for public health insurance while covering a much smaller percentage of the population.

Adding more people to our more-expensive system only deepens the cost gap. There are deeper healthcare-delivery system differences that drive the cost differential between the US and Canada.

How Does Care Delivery Compare?

Because the US healthcare system is so expensive, one might assume that the US has significantly more hospital beds and many more physicians per capita. Wrong! The number of hospital beds per person and physicians per person in the US and in Canada are virtually identical.

- **Point #1: We both have the same number of hospital beds, but utilization in Canada is higher.** Canada has 2.55 hospital beds per 1,000 people, and the US has 2.6. (3) Although the number of hospital beds per person in the US and Canada are virtually identical, the utilization of the healthcare-system capacity is very different. The occupancy of acute hospital beds in Canada was 91.6%, while in the US, it was at 62.8%. Canada had the third-highest hospital-occupancy rate among OECD countries, while the US had the lowest occupancy rate. Canadian hospitals are typically funded through an annual global budget process set in conjunction with the province or territory. There is no financial incentive in Canada to shorten lengths of stay to get people out of the hospital. The US hospital-reimbursement system is primarily a pay-for-volume-of-services system. The American system has focused for decades on shorter lengths of stay; this focus on length of stay has not controlled cost or increased quality outcomes, however.

- **Point #2: Both countries have the same number of physicians, but Canada is primary-care-driven.** The number of physicians per capita is the same in the two countries, with both having 2.6 physicians per 1,000 people. (3) However, the area of focus is vastly different. A physician in Canada is more than four times more likely to be in general practice. The Canadian system is based on dual-purpose primary care, meaning primary care provides (1) the first line of treatment *plus* (2) the coordination of other services to ease movement and ensure continuity of care. The commitment to coordination of care by primary-care physicians is so strong that some provinces pay less to a specialist for non-referred care. The American system often puts the financial penalty on the *patient* when a referral from primary care is not received, while the Canadian system puts the responsibility for the referral on the medical providers.

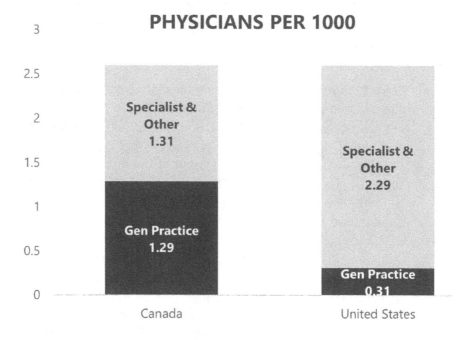

PHYSICIANS PER 1000

Canada: Specialist & Other 1.31, Gen Practice 1.29
United States: Specialist & Other 2.29, Gen Practice 0.31

Source: Organisation for Economic Co-operation and Development. "OECD Health Statistics." OECD Health Data. 2018

- **Point #3: The US is a convenience- and procedure-driven system.** The focus on specialty care and procedures can be seen in a comparison of the number of magnetic resonance imaging (MRI) machines in each country. Americans expect speed and convenience in tests and services related to procedures and specialty care. The US has almost four times the number of MRI machines per person compared to Canada.

MRI MACHINES PER MILLION

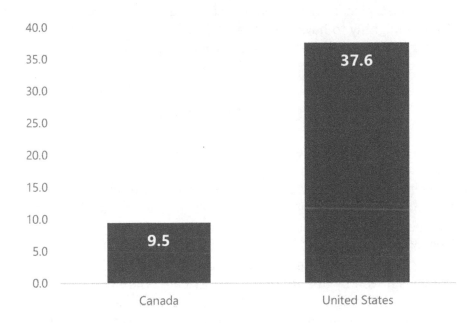

Source: Organisation for Economic Co-operation and Development. "OECD Health Statistics." OECD Health Data. 2018

Better access to specialty care in the US is not just limited to humans. One Saturday afternoon, I found our dachshund, Max, in a chair in our living room, unable to move. I scooped him up and rushed him to the veterinarian. Poor little Max was paralyzed. The veterinarian said it was likely a slipped disc that was creating spinal compression and that we might be able to save Max if we could find the exact cause. The vet said he could send us to an emergency veterinary clinic for an MRI. Max was my daughter's dog, so off I went to the emergency vet!

Max was immediately taken in for an MRI. Sure enough, the diagnosis was confirmed: Max had a slipped disc that had caused a compression of his spinal cord, leading him to become paralyzed. It was either emergency spinal surgery or euthanasia for Max. Did I mention he was my daughter's dog? Emergency spinal surgery it was! Within one hour of becoming paralyzed, Max the dachshund, had had an MRI. Within three hours, he was in surgery to relieve the compression on his spinal cord.

In most places in the world, including Canada, people would struggle mightily to have this level of care access, and we have it for our dogs. This level of access and convenience in the US comes at a cost.

Putting It All Together

Politicians will sometimes use the lower cost and better outcomes of the Canadian system as rationales for a universal public healthcare financing system, aka Medicare for all. It is essential to understand that the Canadian system, which covers all Canadians, has a lower cost per capita than our government programs, which cover only 36% of the population. The difference in structure of delivery may be bigger than the difference in insurance funding. The Canadian system is driven by dual-purpose primary care. The American system is built on procedures and specialty care. A conversion to a Canadian-style healthcare system would require not only a change in insurance funding but also a fundamental shift in physician authority to primary care and away from facilities and specialists. Creating an American dual-purpose primary-care system would take decades to achieve, but I believe the juice may be worth the squeeze.

We must find a way to improve the quality outcomes of the healthcare system, improve the health and clinical compliance of the population, and lower the cost for all public and private programs. Insurance companies are not in a position to create this change. Hospitals are paid to perform procedures and, therefore, have a conflict of interest in achieving these goals. I believe investment in high-quality primary care is the best hope for positive evolution of our healthcare system.

How would I do it? First, I will remind you that I am not a physician, so I feel woefully inadequate to explain how and why high-performing primary-care physicians outperform others. However, I do know some physicians and physician groups achieve superior patient outcomes and are better able to motivate their patients to manage their medical conditions. A physician can provide an accurate diagnosis and prescribe the best course of treatment, but ultimately, the patient must learn to manage their condition based on the doctor's recommendation. Whether it is better diagnoses, better treatment recommendations, or better communication skills that better motivate patients, we see positive patient variances in some high-performing primary-care groups in our health benefit consulting data analysis.

If I were the healthcare czar, here's what I would do:

- **Empower Dual-Purpose Primary Care**—I would move the care-management dollars within the healthcare financing system to high-performing primary-care physicians who would become responsible for managing the population health of their patients.

- **Measure Dual-Purpose Primary Care**—Primary-care physicians and physician groups would have specific prevention, care-compliance, total-cost, and customer-satisfaction measures. The measures would be available to consumers and would be used to adjust payments. Better-performing physician groups would receive more money than poor performers.

- **Create the Measures**—As czar, I would go to high-performing physicians to learn how to measure physicians. I would start with physicians like Dr. Christopher Crow—an innovator and pioneer in primary care—in North Texas or groups like the Family Medicine Education Consortium, who are working on a primary-care-for-all initiative. Rather than having the government, insurance companies, or hospitals define primary-care quality, I would go to the best primary-care physicians and ask them how to do it. After the group of the highest-performing physicians designed the plan, government, insurance companies, and hospitals could implement it and align their behaviors and actions to meet the primary-care measures.

- **Use Five-, Ten-, and Twenty-Year Milestones**—Converting our healthcare system from a procedure-focused system to a dual-purpose primary-care system can't happen overnight because we simply don't have enough primary-care physicians. In addition, the financial disruption of aggressively moving the authority to primary care is problematic. The primary-care group described in the previous point would be responsible

for creating a five-year plan that effectively moved financial, authority, and data resources to primary care. The ten-year plan would have specific prevention, care compliance, and quality outcomes. The twenty-year plan would include a generational flip in our medical training and residencies to produce a specific target number and percentage of primary-care physicians.

The goal of a dual-purpose program would be to provide every American with access to high-performing primary care to help them prevent disease, find and treat medical conditions earlier, and navigate the healthcare system in urgent, complex, or comorbid events. Advances in technology may catapult us forward regarding timely and proper diagnosis, but proper diagnosis without patient education, engagement, motivation, and navigation will struggle to advance quality outcomes. High-performing primary care can provide the education, engagement, motivation, and navigation required to help patients improve results.

The Case for Canada for All

Canada covers all citizens at a fraction of the cost of the US, and its people live longer. Universal coverage, lower cost, and longer lives sound pretty good to me.

The Argument Against Canada for All

The primary-care-based infrastructure of the Canadian healthcare system creates different stakeholder motivations than the American procedure-based system. Covering all Americans with a government-funded universal health insurance program without altering the underlying health-system structure would solve the uninsured problem, but the cost and quality variances between the US and Canada would remain.

Sources

(1)   "Health Care in Canada." Canada.ca.

(2)   The Commonwealth Fund. "International Health Care System Profiles." International.commonwealthfund.org. 2019.

(3)   Organisation for Economic Co-operation and Development. "OECD Health Statistics." OECD Health Data. 2018.

Chapter 20:

Universal Coverage—Is Healthcare a Right or Responsibility?

THE ACA GUARANTEED UNIVERSAL ACCESS to health insurance for everyone in America. No one can be denied health insurance coverage, but the ACA came up far short of guaranteeing universal coverage. Universal coverage simply means that every person has health insurance. It does not mean the insurance is free, and it does not mean that the insurance must be delivered through a public program. It simply means everyone has coverage.

Should every person in the US have health insurance coverage? Even the most politically conservative person would likely answer that it would be a good thing if every person had health insurance. The more relevant question for the political debate is if every person in the US *must* have health insurance coverage. Your answer to this question is heavily influenced by how you reply in the pop quiz.

Pop Quiz

Choose all that you believe apply.

Healthcare is a _____.

    (1) right

    (2) privilege

    (3) responsibility

    (4) choice

    (5) mandate

How our elected members of Congress and the president fill in the blank will determine the future of healthcare in America.

Healthcare Is a Right?

The Constitution of the World Health Organization states that "the highest attainable standard of health is one of the fundamental rights of every human being." The WHO constitution was written in 1946. Its modern interpretation is that every person has a human right to healthcare services, without regard to status or ability to pay. Although the US is a member country of the WHO, as a sovereign nation, the US is not subject to the WHO constitution. However, some believe this standard should apply to the US.

The Declaration of Independence defines the inalienable rights of life, liberty, and the pursuit of happiness. Thomas Jefferson did not include health insurance in his list of inalienable rights, but are life, liberty, and the pursuit of happiness jeopardized by a lack of health insurance? An honest assessment is sobering. Life is jeopardized by a lack of health insurance. Disease detection and treatment may exist but can be out of reach without insurance. Remember the T. rex effect from earlier in the book? Your individual pursuit of happiness is clearly impacted by your physical and mental health. Living with complications from untreated disease or chronic illness can ruin one's entire existence. A case could be made that health insurance coverage and the access to the healthcare system it creates are critical elements of Thomas Jefferson's written rights to life, liberty, and the pursuit of happiness.

Those holding campaign signs that read "Healthcare Is a Right!" probably are not thinking about the WHO constitution or the Declaration of Independence. I believe they are saying that it is the government's responsibility to guarantee each individual person's right to healthcare services. When we say this is the land of the free, do we now mean free healthcare? If healthcare is a right, do I have a responsibility to pay for it? If I exercise my right to not purchase coverage, what rights do I have to access public care when needed, and what responsibility do other taxpayers have to pay for it?

"Healthcare Is a Right!" may be easy to paint on a campaign sign, but the statement carries massive political, economic, and social implications.

Healthcare Is a Privilege?

The question "Is healthcare a right or a privilege?" contains a powerful political trap. In ways, it is similar to the question "Have you stopped beating your dog?" If I answer yes to the latter question, it implies that I was previously beating my dog. If I answer no, it implies that I was, and still am, beating my dog. The question itself traps me in my answer.

I do not believe anyone would rightfully argue that healthcare is a privilege for only the wealthy or powerful. A privilege is not the opposite of, or the only alternative to, a right. As much as I disdain the entrapping nature of the question, there is much to be learned from it. Health insurance prevalence and access to healthcare services vary across socioeconomic lines. These variances lead to health-outcome differentials in the US based on economic means. The question about whether health insurance is a privilege is really a condemnation of the economic discrimination that exists in today's healthcare system. Smart politicians will pay attention to the underlying messages of income-based healthcare inequality in the question.

Healthcare Is a Responsibility?

A right typically has a corresponding responsibility. I have the right to liberty, but my liberty stops when it infringes upon someone else's liberty. Our legal foundation is built upon respecting, and not treading upon, others' rights and freedoms. Rights must be balanced by corresponding responsibilities. An infant has rights without responsibilities because the infant is not yet capable of understanding or meeting responsibilities. An infant has a right to be fed and cared for. No one would expect a newborn infant to feed and care for itself. The baby does not have the physical, psychological, or economic capacity to feed and care for itself. Fair responsibility only exists where the capacity to meet the expectation exists.

Who, then, has the financial capacity to pay for healthcare? This question applies to the federal and state governments and also applies to individual households. Politicians talk about a single-payer system, but sometimes I think Americans simply want an "other-payer" system. They want the healthcare system that someone else funds! Expanding public health insurance coverage without the revenue increases to cover it meets today's social responsibility to the public health insurance recipients, but it is fiscally irresponsible for future taxpayers who must pay for today's expenditures plus interest. Future taxpayers should not be the "other payer" for today's public health insurance programs. The ACA Medicaid expansion and Marketplace subsidies were designed to offset the cost of health insurance to allow individuals to affordably meet their coverage responsibilities. Is healthcare expensive? Yes, but the public programs provide a bridge to affordability. The reality is, we have a responsibility to improve the financial efficiency of healthcare to allow society and individual households to meet their responsibilities to pay it.

Healthcare Is a Choice?

The ACA made health insurance coverage a choice with guaranteed availability because no one could be denied coverage. However, individuals still have the choice whether to purchase health insurance. A universal-coverage plan built on the belief that healthcare is a right effectively removes the choice to not have health insurance coverage.

By definition, a plan that covers everyone cannot allow the freedom of choice for an individual to not have coverage. Those who want universal coverage and also want freedom of choice to opt out really do not want universal *coverage*; they want universal *access*, which is what the ACA already has created. You cannot have both universal coverage and choice if any person makes the choice to not have coverage.

Healthcare Is a Mandate?

The ACA included coverage mandates for individuals and for large employers. Individuals who chose to not purchase health insurance were subject to a tax penalty until the Trump administration reduced the penalty to zero, effective January 1, 2019. Large employers are subject to a penalty if they do not offer health insurance to their full-time employees. The freedom of choice and the mandates are married. The mandates answer the question: "What happens if I don't purchase the required coverage?" Supporting freedom of choice with no mandate means one does not believe in universal health coverage. Those who support universal coverage must determine the appropriate penalty for those who reject the coverage. For the US to reach universal coverage, the mandate and penalty must be greater than the actual cost of coverage. It is illogical and inconsistent to support universal coverage without a strong mandate and penalty for noncompliance.

What's Next?

"Healthcare Is a Right!" will be a popular campaign sign. The broader implications of the slogan will be underanalyzed and rarely, if ever, discussed on television or in a campaign speech. "Healthcare Is a Responsibility!" will not show up on a T-shirt, billboard, or campaign sign. Responsibilities are not politically popular because they turn the focus from what you (the candidate) can do for me (the voter) to what I need to do for myself, my family, my neighbor, my community, and my country.

Section Closing

The array of options between repeal-and-replace on the right and Medicare for all on the left is vast but confusing to many voters. Politicians are typically long on promises and short on details when it comes to healthcare. The gap between what is being promoted on the campaign trail and what is being negotiated in the real world, like in North Carolina, is massive. Politicians are trying to tap into the frustration with America's current health insurance system while many stakeholders are clinging firmly to the status quo. Healthcare represents 17.9% of the entire US economy and directly accounts for one of every nine jobs. It is easy to get votes with a three-word healthcare slogan, but truly solving our cost, coverage, complexity, and quality healthcare crises is infinitely more complicated.

SECTION 4:

RECOMMENDED COURSE OF TREATMENT

MY ORIGINAL WORKING TITLE FOR this book was *I Can Fix Healthcare*. My move away from that title was not a lightning bolt of humility or the death of my Texas bravado. I simply came to understand that trying to solve a problem without first helping the reader to identify and understand the problem was misplaced effort and was ultimately fruitless. On the other side of the argument, leaving readers without my recommendations feels cowardly. It is easy to shine a light on the current system's shortcomings and to provide a critique of current political options without the risk of offending stakeholders. Actually making recommendations exposes you to criticism because you move from being the dart thrower to becoming the dartboard. The patient (the US healthcare system) cannot afford silence, inaction, and cowardice. The dartboard is on the wall, so let's hit the bull's-eye!

In this book, we have become familiar with the patient by learning about the current programs. We diagnosed the causes of the major cost, complexity, and quality symptoms. We have listened to the politician specialists to understand the treatment options currently being proposed. It is time to make a decision. No action means no improvement, and I believe no improvement is an American tragedy. This section outlines my priorities and suggested course of treatment for America's healthcare system.

Chapter 21:

Let's Role!

YES, I KNOW THAT'S NORMALLY not how *roll* is spelled in this context. However, the beginning of the healthcare fix is to clarify the roles of all stakeholders toward a common goal.

Step 1: Identify the Enemy

Everyone knows the problems, but opinions vary greatly on who, or what, is to blame for our healthcare system's shortcomings. Republicans blame Democrats. Democrats blame Republicans. Hospitals blame insurance companies. Insurance companies blame hospitals. Primary-care physicians blame specialists. Specialists blame noncompliant patients. Patients blame gluten! The blame game is alive and well, but it is a fool's game. The real enemy is sitting in the background, continuing its assault on the American people and the American economy while the stakeholders point the finger of blame toward one another.

So, who is the villain? Disease! The time, energy, and money spent blaming other stakeholders should instead be focused on fighting disease. The problem is not Republicans, Democrats, insurance companies, hospitals, doctors, pharmaceutical companies, or even gluten. The problem is that we produce too much disease in this country too early in our lives, and it is too expensive and too hard to get the care we need to get better. The problem is not too much healthcare; it is too much disease . . . and I *hate* disease!

If you have ever heard these words, then you hate disease, too:

- "It's malignant."

- "You have diabetes."

- "We are going to have to operate."

- "Somebody call an ambulance!"

- "Is there a pulse?"

- "Can we stop the bleeding?"

- "There is no known cure."

These words teleport the patient, their family, and their support group into an alternate reality. You are immediately in a place you don't recognize. The words and language are unfamiliar. Suddenly, you have swapped your favorite jeans for a paper gown with inadequate backside coverage. The disease that teleports you to this new reality is the enemy. To borrow from the New Testament's book of John, who is the thief (enemy) who comes to steal, kill, and destroy? The enemy in healthcare is disease! It steals your money. It can alter your mind and steal your memories. It disables you. It can literally kill you.

Never forget, disease is the enemy that all stakeholders in the healthcare system are trying to defeat. The cost and complexity problems within the healthcare system create a massive distraction that steals focus, resources, and attention from the true enemy.

Step 2: Know Your Role

In my speaking events, I will put a picture of a cinnamon roll up on the screen and ask the audience what it is. They confidently respond, "Cinnamon roll." I then put up a picture of a roll of toilet paper, which they can also easily identify. My final image is of a Tootsie Roll, which is even easier to identify because the name is emblazoned on the packaging. The point of this identification exercise is to let the audience understand that these are all rolls but that not all rolls serve the same purpose. Warming up toilet paper to eat for breakfast would not be very satisfying . . . and please don't enter the bathroom carrying a bag of Tootsie Rolls! Each roll is great when it fulfills its designed role and purpose.

Different roles in healthcare exist, and each is important, but each stakeholder must fill its appropriate role. I hope you agree that disease is the true enemy of the healthcare system and that all stakeholders need to align to make war against cancer, diabetes, cardiovascular disease, and other diseases of mass destruction. The problem comes when there is a lack of role clarity or when a stakeholder assumes the wrong role. Role confusion leads to inefficiency, high cost, poor quality, and conflict. A key to correctly reforming healthcare is appropriately identifying and assigning the right roles to the right stakeholders.

Roles in Healthcare

The primary roles in healthcare are finance, care delivery, and administration.

- **Finance**—The finance role deals with how everything in healthcare is funded. What is financed through taxes, and who pays those taxes? How are required premiums determined? How much should employers contribute toward healthcare costs? How much financial responsibility should employees/voters/patients/members/individuals have? What is the appropriate price for healthcare services? What level of price discrimination is acceptable? What wellness or compliance incentives are appropriate, and for whom?

- **Care Delivery**—The care-delivery role deals with what care is appropriate and how it is accessed, by whom and for whom. What is considered an appropriate treatment, and what is experimental? Who determines the actual course of treatment? Who helps a patient navigate the system when specialty services are needed? Who defines care-quality measures and standards? Who decides what is and is not covered by insurance?

- **Administration**—The administration role deals with efficiency, education, and the customer experience. How does an individual choose and enroll in a health plan? Who provides the infrastructure for a claim transaction? Who bills and collects premiums and cost sharing? Who handles dispute resolution? Who handles the consumer and provider questions?

The current healthcare system is made up of a combination of public and private programs delivered through an array of public, not-for-profit, and for-profit providers and administrators. Each program has its own set of finance, care delivery, and administrative rules. Not only that, programs vary wildly across state lines and among individual administrators. Essentially, healthcare in the US lacks a consistent benchmark or standard for almost everything. Role clarity leads to cost efficiency and improved results. Unfortunately, role clarity is sorely lacking in our system, which results in high cost and poor outcomes.

Stakeholder Assignments

Healthcare accounted for 17.9% of GDP in 2017. This equates to $10,739 per person. (1) Multiply that by the number of people in your household, and you get what your family's annual economic value is to the healthcare system. The dollars are staggering. The massive money creates a strong incentive for current stakeholders to protect the status quo with all their might. It might not be status quo for the entire healthcare system, but stakeholders want to protect as much status quo as possible for their part of the system.

Here's an example: Hospitals might be okay with a move from employer-sponsored health insurance to individual products. However, they want to maintain private-insurance reimbursement rates for these products rather than have the rates based on Medicare reimbursement levels. It is easy to support change when it is change for someone else!

Can we agree that:

- the coming entitlement mountain of debt is a problem for our country;

- our percentage of GDP spent on healthcare decreases our global economic competitiveness;

- healthcare expenses driving families into bankruptcy is bad;

- having patients go without needed care or medicine because of cost concerns is heartbreaking;

- basing access to care solely on one's ability to pay feels heartless;

- and having the highest death rate for conditions that could have been detected and treated within the existing healthcare system is unacceptable?

If we can agree on these things, then we must be willing to abandon the status quo. All of us must be willing to do so. The questions then become "How invasive is the required change?" and "What is the best way for America to align all stakeholders to win the war on disease?"

Government—Those on the extreme right sometimes think government is the root of all problems, especially in healthcare. Those on the extreme left sometimes think government is the only solution to healthcare's problems. The government provides insurance coverage for more than one-third of Americans and accounts for approximately 50% of total healthcare spending. In addition, the government makes all the rules. Government is permanently and inextricably embedded in America's healthcare system. The properly aligned role of the government includes the following:

- **Safety Net**—The government should provide the social safety net for those who cannot otherwise afford or access healthcare.

- **Price Benchmark**—The government should establish the baseline payment system upon which all healthcare payments are based. It is impossible to create the appropriate transparency, simplicity, and affordability that is needed without a consistent pricing benchmark. A benchmark already exists through Medicare pricing . . . let's go!

- **Quality Benchmark**—The government should facilitate the establishment of consistent care appropriateness and care-quality measures. Different measures and incentives created by individual payers create chaos and confusion for medical providers. Although never perfect, the government is the best source for consistent quality-measure development.

- **Rules of the Road**—Health insurance and healthcare are a public social service delivered by a combination of for-profit, not-for-profit, and public entities. The government must establish the rules of the road to protect consumers clinically and financially.

The government needs to stay out of administration. Outstanding customer-service innovation and quality is not a hallmark of government services. The IRS is the "single-payer" service provider for our tax system; it is not known for its timeliness, friendliness, or positive customer experience. Do we really want a similar level of customer-service accountability in our healthcare?

Medical Providers—Medical providers sometimes feel like they live in a "Mother, may I?" world where they must seek approval before applying their expertise. This leads to unnecessary expense (through defensive medicine), unnecessary administration, and unnecessary delays in treatment. The complicated plan design and reimbursement mechanisms have turned medical providers into part-time collection agencies. A physician might be categorized as four-star by one insurance company and two-star by another because the data and quality measures differ by payer. All this increases cost and creates confusion and a distraction for medical professionals.

Trained and licensed medical professionals should be empowered to care for patients and be held accountable for the results. This means medical professionals should control:

- patient course-of-treatment recommendations,

- patient care navigation, and

- patient case and care management.

Medical providers need relief from the inconsistent billing, claim-payment, and collection processes so they can focus on being the frontline leaders in the battle against disease.

Insurance Companies—Insurance companies are a convenient target of criticism for healthcare's woes. Insurance companies play an important role in administering healthcare. These entities even provide the administration for public programs like Medicare and Medicaid. The frustration for consumers and medical providers rises when the insurance companies come between patients and providers. When your doctor tells you that you need a specific treatment and your insurance company then tells you they won't approve it, who are you going to blame? In most instances, the insurance company becomes the object of the rage. Insurance companies provide an important service in preventing fraud, abuse, and inappropriate treatments; however, there is a fine line between being the advocate who is protecting the patient and being a gatekeeper who keeps patients from getting the care their doctors say they need.

Insurance companies should control:

- the administration of the financial transaction between the patient and provider;

- data aggregation to measure, report, and positively influence quality;

- enrollment and education services;

- customer service; and

- dispute resolution.

Insurance companies should shift the responsibility and funding for care management and care navigation to medical providers who are accountable for the results. Think of it this way: If your doctor's office calls or your insurance company calls, which one are you going to answer? The appropriate role for an insurance company is not to determine the course of treatment; it is to measure, reward, and report quality results so medical consumers can make informed decisions. The quality measurements should be consistent across all payers.

Employers—Employers are a key financial stakeholder because they pay for so much of the healthcare for their employees and through Medicare taxes. The replacement of the current system with a government-run Medicare-for-all system would not change the financing role employers would play; it would simply flip the payment responsibility from premiums and claims to taxes.

The link between health insurance and employment has broader economic implications that go well beyond healthcare. There is a link between employment and the availability of entitlement programs. Some on the right referred to Obamacare as a job killer. In fact, one Republican repeal-and-replace bill was called H.R.2—Repealing the Job-Killing Health Care Law Act. Some on the left claimed Obamacare had killed job lock and that Americans no longer had to work to get affordable health insurance. The CBO provided analysis in the job killer vs. job lock debate. Analysis from the CBO concluded that the labor force will shrink by approximately two million people as a result of the ACA. This reduction is not because employers will eliminate jobs but because fewer people choose to work because of the public coverage expansions in the ACA.

So, was the ACA a job killer or did it eliminate job lock? Both answers are equally correct and incorrect.

- **ACA as a Job Killer**—The ACA did not eliminate jobs, but it did eliminate workers. The presence of a government subsidy for health insurance and the ability to obtain individual health insurance with no preexisting-condition limitations removed a motivation for some people to work. The result is that because of the ACA, fewer Americans are choosing to work.

- **ACA Eliminates Job Lock**—The ACA individual-insurance reforms allow people to leave job or change jobs without the fear of losing insurability because of preexisting medical conditions.

I believe the American economy needs incentives to keep people working. Economic growth is inextricably linked to growth in the available labor pool. A properly aligned, designed, and funded employer-sponsored health-insurance system provides a strong incentive for workers to freely choose to remain in the labor pool. Remember, employers will be a primary funding source for *any* US healthcare system, so the question becomes whether the employers and the economy get an increased labor pool from this investment.

Chapter Quiz

Select the answer that best aligns with your belief.

A. Health insurance should be linked to employment and should provide an incentive for individuals to work, as well as a positive stimulant to the labor-participation rate.

B. Health insurance should not be linked to employment, and any negative impact to the labor-participation rate is a separate economic issue.

The appropriate role for employers goes well beyond simply paying for healthcare's dinner. The employer role in healthcare should include:

- administrative support in enrollment and communication;

- financial support for covered employees and families;

- appropriate wellness incentives to encourage prevention and early detection; and

- connection with medical professionals.

Employers need relief from the weighty regulatory requirements and discriminatory pricing of the current system.

Patients, Members, Employees, Voters, Individuals . . . YOU!—What is your role and responsibility in healthcare? The same question applies to your coworkers, your neighbors, your family members, and every other person in America. Trying to successfully navigate a collusive financial system on our own does not work for many of us. That said, there is no "free" healthcare system. We cannot be free from financial responsibility, free from health responsibility, and free from personal responsibility. We have a responsibility to pay our share of healthcare costs up to some affordability measure, a responsibility to take care of ourselves, and a responsibility to follow our physician's recommended courses of treatment. If we don't accept our individual responsibility, who else is responsible for funding our irresponsibility? You will likely not see "Healthcare Is a Responsibility!" signs at a campaign rally, but we will ultimately have to put politics aside to create a system that includes appropriate individual responsibility.

Your role in healthcare should include:

- the *right* to healthcare coverage and treatment that is not based on your ability to pay, and

- the *responsibility* to financially contribute based on your ability to pay, to exercise reasonable self-care, and to comply with your treating physician's recommended course of treatment.

Now that we have agreed how to perfectly align the stakeholder roles, feel free to go get a Tootsie Pop and let me know how many licks it really takes to get to the center. The world may never know how many licks it takes, but America should know how all stakeholders are willing to set aside the status quo to create a more affordable and more effective healthcare system that aligns itself to defeat disease.

Source

(1)   Centers for Medicare and Medicaid Services. "National Health Expenditures, Table 21. Expenditures, Enrollment and Per Enrollee Estimate of Health Insurance: United States, Calendar Years 1987–2017." Cms.gov. April 26, 2019.

Chapter 22:

Priority 1—Sustain Medicare

MEDICARE IS THE SINGLE LARGEST purchaser of healthcare services in the US. This fact alone makes Medicare extremely influential in healthcare. However, Medicare has some serious financial struggles. The combination of healthcare inflation and the declining ratio of workers to Medicare beneficiaries puts the solvency of Medicare in jeopardy. Nobody wants to see Medicare go away . . . okay, so Bernie Sanders does want to eliminate Medicare as we know it so he can steal the name. The first priority in my recommended course of treatment for the American healthcare system is to sustain Medicare.

Medicare-Centric Healthcare

I do not only want to sustain Medicare, my recommendation is to make healthcare in America Medicare-centric. Medicare could, and should, be the hub upon which all other healthcare programs spin. This is far from a Medicare-for-all recommendation. Medicare-centric means all other programs base their payment methodologies and quality measurements on Medicare.

- **Payment Indexing**—The majority of the political debate surrounding healthcare cost is around *who* pays for it. Is it the consumer, the employer, the government, the wealthy, subsidies, etc.? The cost problem is less about who then *how much*. An even more important topic is payment reform—what we pay for and how we pay for it. We simply pay too much for healthcare services in the privately insured market. Medicare should be the payment standard upon which all other payments are indexed. As previously stated in this book, I have major concerns about the potentially catastrophic economic impact of aligning all medical reimbursements into Medicare. However, I do believe an organized, systematic, and time-specific Medicare balance-billing limit could lower health insurance cost, increase market competition, and simplify the experience for patients and providers without crushing the economy or access to medical services.

- **Quality Benchmark**—Medicare should create the provider quality measures and the payment incentives linked to these measures. An example of Medicare's role in measuring and influencing quality is the Hospital Readmissions Reduction Program. The goal of the program was to lower cost and improve healthcare quality by penalizing payments to hospitals for certain hospital readmissions. The result of this payment program was a reduction in hospital readmissions without creating an increase in outpatient or emergency department visits or patient mortality. (1) Most would say the program was a rousing success, with decreased cost and decreased hospital stays without measurable adverse effects. The American Hospital Association (AHA) communicates a different view of the program: "The Affordable Care Act (ACA) required the Centers for Medicare and Medicaid Services (CMS) to penalize hospitals for 'excess' readmissions when compared to 'expected' levels of readmissions. Since the start of the program on Oct. 1, 2012, hospitals have experienced nearly $1.9 billion of penalties, including $528 million in fiscal year (FY) 2017." (2) The AHA does not love the program as designed and would like sociodemographic factors to be added. Refining the measurement may be appropriate, but the bottom line is that behaviors change when reimbursements are tied to specific measures. Rather than creating competing incentives, all payers should align quality measures and incentives with Medicare.

I am cautious about recommending Medicare-eligibility expansion. My belief on this is more precautionary than a pure prohibition. Adding eligible populations without solving Medicare's financially cloudy future is fiscally irresponsible. The federal government has a poor history of adequately funding major health programs, leading to deficit and debt problems over time. Solving health insurance affordability by expanding Medicare eligibility in the near term while deepening our long-term debt problem feels like the medical equivalent of trading heart failure for terminal cancer. We need to both make health insurance more affordable *and* adequately finance Medicare. The Medicare-centric approach builds on Medicare's strengths without further burdening its economic future.

Increasing Medicare Revenue

Medicare needs more money. I can't say it any more clearly. The ideal solution creates additional revenue for Medicare *without* increasing Medicare's expenses or liabilities. Here's how we could do this:

Employer-Sponsored Tax Exemption

The tax deduction for employer-sponsored health insurance is the largest tax expenditure in the Internal Revenue Code and is projected to be worth $4.2 trillion over the ten-year period of 2020–2029. (3) The value of the deduction includes the employer and employee deductibility. It is not only corporate money; it is also your paycheck.

As a consultant who works to help employers lower the cost and improve the quality of their health-benefit plans, how could I possibly recommend touching the employer tax deduction? In conjunction with the other changes, I believe the tax deduction could be capped, creating revenue for Medicare without increasing costs to companies or their employees, and I also believe it would not lead to a decrease in the number or percentage of employers offering health insurance coverage.

- **Step 1: Cap the Deduction**—The federal subsidy for the tax deduction is worth $283 billion in 2019 and grows to $562 billion in 2029. This is a 99% growth in the value of the deduction based solely on cost growth. The CBO projects that 159 million people will have employer-sponsored health coverage in 2020 and ten years later. Freezing the deduction at the 2019 level creates a tax expenditure savings of $1.4 trillion over ten years that could be directed risk-free and expense-free to Medicare to maintain its solvency.

Freezing the deduction is an interesting intellectual exercise, but it would be difficult to administer. If the deduction were capped at 80% rather than 100% of health-plan costs, the savings over ten years would be $836 billion. Employers and taxpayers are not going to volunteer for this reduction, but maintaining Medicare solvency can't be extended without changes somewhere.

- **Step 2: Penalty Equal to Cost**—Continued cost increases and a cap on the deduction described in Step 1 could suppress employer offer rates of health insurance. This would lead to an increase in the number of uninsured Americans and an increase in the government coverage and subsidies through other programs. The net government subsidy cost per subsidized person in the ACA Marketplace is $6,490 in 2019 and is projected to grow to $11,670 in 2029. (4) The penalty for a large employer who does not offer health insurance coverage is $2,320 per full-time employee (minus the first thirty employees). (5) A penalty of $2,320 per employee gets nowhere near covering the net subsidy cost of $6,490 per person. The net subsidy for a family of four in the Obamacare Marketplace is $25,960. The federal government must keep large employers in the health insurance game, and a penalty that is closer to the net subsidy cost removes the exit motivation for an employer.

- **Step 3: Network Access Fee**—Those covered by private insurance would enjoy a potentially significant reduction in health insurance premiums if provider reimbursements were indexed to Medicare. A small portion of the savings could be charged as a network access fee payable to Medicare. Every private insurance program would pay the network access fee. The health insurance industry would refer to this type of program as shared savings. (In shared savings, an insurance plan saves money and pays back a portion of the savings through an administrative fee.)

This Medicare-centric approach could help financially sustain Medicare while reducing costs for private insurance plans and reducing administrative and quality measurement complexity for medical providers.

Sources

(1) MedPAC. "The Hospital Readmissions Reduction Program Has Succeeded for Beneficiaries and the Medicare Program." Medpac. gov. June 15, 2018.

(2) American Hospital Association. "Factsheet Hospital Readmissions Reduction Program." Aha.org. January 2018.

(3) Congressional Budget Office. "Federal Subsidies for Health Insurance. Table 2-1 Net Federal Subsidies Associated with Health Insurance Coverage, 2019–2029." Cbo.gov. May 2019.

(4) Congressional Budget Office. "Federal Subsidies for Health Insurance." Cbo.gov. May 2019.

(5) Cigna. "Employer Mandate Fact Sheet." Cigna.com. June 2018.

Chapter 23:

Priority 2—Protect Access

THE ACA GUARANTEED ACCESS TO health insurance for every American. No one can be turned down for health insurance. The law came up short of universal coverage because not everyone has chosen to buy health insurance, but it did meet its goal of universal access to insurance. For me, access is more than just insurance; access means the healthcare system is healthy enough to meet the needs of the population. Access to insurance that financially cripples the healthcare-delivery system is really no access at all; it is like having a gift card to a store that is closed. Any changes to the financing of the healthcare system need to adequately fund the entire system to guarantee access to what I believe are the best medical providers in the world.

Access to Insurance

The ACA's prohibitions against medical underwriting and its preexisting-condition protections should be continued. Actions to protect access to insurance vary by source of insurance coverage.

- **Medicare**—Maintain Medicare's age sixty-five eligibility. Increasing the eligibility age exposes more individuals to the individual insurance market at the highest-cost ages.

Decreasing Medicare's eligibility age potentially exposes Medicare to additional inadequately funded membership. Sustaining Medicare is Step 1 in the course of treatment for the healthcare system.

- **Medicaid**—Whether it is through Medicare block grants or some other grand compromise between the federal government and the non-expansion states, we must find a way to extend health insurance coverage for the lowest-income individuals in our society.

- **Employer-Sponsored Insurance**—Aligning the non-offer penalty more closely with the government subsidy expense would keep large-employer money in healthcare. Small employers are exempt from the ACA mandate. The percentage of small employers offering health insurance pales in comparison to large employers. Adding taxes, fees, or expenses to small businesses is about as politically popular as picking on the middle class. Ouch! I have to rip the Band-Aid off on this one. I understand politically why the Obama administration granted this small-business exemption; however, this exemption contributes to America's uninsured problem. The large-employer penalty is not a tax because it is in no way linked to profitability. The introduction of a small-business health-responsibility fee linked to profits for those who did not offer health insurance might be a way to encourage small-business health-insurance offer rates without stifling investment and innovation.

- **Individual Market**—Individuals purchasing nonsubsidized health insurance are pooled with those purchasing health insurance primarily with government subsidies. The subsidized market is a public insurance program using the private insurance platform. These private programs reimburse medical providers at rates that are significantly higher than public-program reimbursements, on average. This results in poor value for the covered individuals and for the taxpayers funding the subsidies. Public-program provider-reimbursement levels should be used for public programs, and the subsidized Marketplace is a public program.

Transitioning the Marketplace to public-program reimbursement rates could be accomplished in several ways.

One method would be to have insurance carriers use Medicare reimbursement rates for subsidized plan enrollment. Another method would be to use Medicaid as the delivery vehicle for the subsidized plans. Medicaid has experienced the lowest rate of inflation over the last decade, while the individual market has had the highest rate of inflation. I refer to this approach as Medicaid Light. A third approach would be a public-plan option that reimburses at Medicare rates.

Separating the subsidized and nonsubsidized individual markets creates a path for consumerism to work. When all participants in the individual market are using their own money to purchase health insurance, the market has a chance to become an efficient consumer market. I believe we would see substantial decreases in premiums under this approach, especially if it is combined with Medicare indexing for the pricing of medical services. The Internal Revenue Code discriminates against this group compared to those who purchase health insurance through their employers. I would equalize tax treatment of this group of taxpayers with those who purchase through their employers. A cap on the employer-sponsored tax exemption would help facilitate this tax equalization.

Access to Care

Guaranteeing access to health insurance is meaningless if the financial viability of the healthcare delivery system is damaged. We must lower the cost of healthcare services, but I believe we need to be extremely cautious in how we decrease reimbursements and funding for the healthcare industry to protect access to healthcare services.

Indexing reimbursements to what Medicare pays allows the healthcare system to adjust to lower prices over time. Effectively, we let air out of the healthcare economic balloon slowly and systematically rather than popping it. A balance-billing limit of 200% of Medicare for facility payments and 150% for professional services could be a start. A more aggressive 160% and 130% could also be the starting point. I am less concerned about how much air we let out of the balloon initially than I am about getting the exhalation process started with a time-specific, predetermined outcome. Simply squeezing medical-provider reimbursements feels like an inadequate approach. The comprehensive reform needs to adequately insure more Americans so providers spend less time and money chasing patient payments and absorbing bad debt. It must also streamline administrative and quality-measurement requirements so providers can improve efficiency and lower the administrative cost of doing business.

When put together in a coordinated fashion, these steps will allow us to walk forward while protecting access to insurance protection and to healthcare services.

Chapter 24:

Priority 3—Lower Cost . . . for Everyone

HEALTHCARE COST IS CAPTURED IN a simple formula:

Price

x Use

= Cost

If we want to lower the cost of healthcare, we must either lower the price we pay for every unit of healthcare purchased or reduce the number of healthcare units purchased. Example: To lower the cost of hospital inpatient services, you lower either the price you pay per day of hospitalization or the number of days of hospitalization purchased. Simple, right? The formula is easy to understand, but effectively lowering price and utilization is difficult.

Start with Use

The Canadian healthcare system covers every person in Canada for far less cost than our government system, which covers only 36% of the population. Adding in the cost for the majority of Americans who purchase private health insurance makes the cost gap almost laughable. I am not saying we need to flip a switch, start watching hockey, and implement a Canadian-style system. However, I do believe there is much we can learn from Canada's dual-purpose primary-care model that could be successfully implemented over time in the US.

The power in healthcare follows the money, and the money is aligned with facilities and specialists. We have a procedure-based economic model; we need to evolve to a model based on prevention, detection, and high-value health navigation.

I entered the health insurance business in the late 1980s, when this new thing called a PPO was being introduced and health maintenance organizations (HMOs) were gaining market share. By the mid-1990s, I was delivering flat renewals and rate decreases to our HMO customers. The mighty HMOs had killed healthcare inflation! Ultimately, patients in many parts of the country resisted the perceived restrictive networks and approval systems of the HMOs, and inflation returned to healthcare.

As a young insurance salesperson, I was confused by the HMO capitation payments to primary-care physicians (PCPs). The HMO was paying a fixed amount of money per month (capitation) to the PCP whether the patient received any healthcare services. There was little-to-no volatility in the PCP claim expenses even without a capitation. I wondered why our insurance company was making a fixed payment for services that had almost no cost volatility. What I missed at the time was the key role that effective primary care can have in controlling cost and quality variability throughout the entire healthcare system. It wasn't control of the 5 cents spent with the PCP that mattered—it was the positive influence that an effective PCP could have on the remaining 95 cents of every dollar!

In the early days of HMOs, you signed up with a PCP when you enrolled in insurance. That practice has largely been eliminated. The high-performing Canadian system has invested heavily in access to primary care for its citizens. I believe a shifting of dollars, data, resources, and responsibility to high-performing primary care is the least invasive way to positively transform our medical system. We don't have to copy Canada to improve cost and quality, but we should not ignore what works in their system and has historically worked in ours. A dual-purpose primary-care system appropriately aligns authority and resources to lower cost and improve health outcomes. The evolution of our system toward primary care will take time—decades, to be specific—but I believe it is the best long-term cost- and quality-improvement opportunity.

Price

We have a missing link. Pharmaceutical and medical-provider reimbursements for public and private payers and from the rest of the world are disconnected. We must intentionally connect US pharmaceutical prices to those in the rest of the world. We must also intentionally connect the private-system reimbursements to the public-program reimbursements to protect Americans against unaffordable price discrimination.

Cost Part 1: Pharmacy

The US is home to 4% of the world's population and accounts for 42% of the world's pharmaceutical revenue. The tobacco industry spent more money lobbying in Washington, DC, than any other industry in 1998, and the pharmaceutical industry has been the biggest spender in lobbying efforts over the twenty-one years since 1998. (1) There is a reason they spend so much money on lobbying politicians . . . it works. The American people have been saddled with the cost of an opaque pharmaceutical industry.

Politicians on both sides openly admit their disdain for our pharmaceutical price position among global competitors, but it does not seem like much ever changes. President Trump has made several attempts to battle drug prices. On July 5, 2019, he said he was working on an executive order that would give the US a most-favored nation status on prescription drug pricing, meaning the US would pay the lowest price of any country for a drug. The comments were short on details, but it is clear President Trump is frustrated with the inability of Congress and his administration to make meaningful progress on the drug-price issue.

The pharmaceutical and insurance industries have failed American consumers by consistently charging them more than consumers in other countries for the same prescription drugs. The free market has failed. Did you hear me? The free market has failed American consumers. The government must intercede where the market fails. I am not typically a fan of anything that resembles government price setting, but I do not see a positive free-enterprise path forward. The pharmaceutical industry has been taking as much as it can from as many as it can for as long as it can in America. That is called capitalism, but it is also called greed. The pharmaceutical industry is also providing an amazing social service by creating drugs that can relieve pain, cure disease, and extend life. The cures created by the pharmaceutical industry are amazing, but the price discrimination against Americans is condemning.

My concern over the government's ultimate action on drug pricing is that the government will create a regulated marketplace for public programs and leave private programs unprotected. An example would be the federal government negotiating price caps on Medicare Part D drugs but leaving the individual insurance and employer-sponsored markets out of the legislation. This approach could cause even further cost shifting, resulting in an increase in the cost of prescription drugs in private insurance.

Republicans and Democrats, Congress and the White House, and Hatfields and McCoys need to all put their feuding aside to solve the pharmaceutical price-discrimination crisis faced by the American people.

Cost Part 2: Everything Else

If you have made it this far in the book, then you know my first step in lowering private insurance cost is to index reimbursements to Medicare on a systematic, time-specific basis. This not only lowers cost but also opens the door for increased insurance competition as the medical insurers begin to compete on service, efficiency, and the ability to motivate and connect with participants to deliver measurably improved health outcomes in the population. Today, the negotiation of network discounts creates a barrier to entry for new competition and is the inappropriate focus of too many employer insurance decisions.

Medicare Catastrophic

The second recommended Medicare link is related to catastrophic claim pricing. The federal government administers a national flood insurance program that it initiated because the government felt that the damage and losses from large-scale floods were too great for the private insurance market to absorb. In essence, the government stepped in where it felt the private insurance market was unable to solve the risk problem. The impact of large claims on employers in health insurance can be flood-like.

Most insurance company contracts with hospitals contain "outlier" provisions where the hospital receives a higher reimbursement level for claims over a specified threshold. The result is that payment percentages go up as billed charges increase.

This reimbursement model creates significant perverse financial incentives. Hospitals are incented to raise billed rates without regard to the actual cost of services, to bundle as many services as they can into a single bill to trigger the contract threshold, to perform additional tests and services, and to practice defensive medicine. In a sick twist, the best thing that can happen financially for a hospital is for a patient to have enormous complications.

The perverse billing incentives along with advances in medicine, such as injectable drugs, have combined to increase the prevalence of high-cost medical claims—claims that exceed $1 million in a single year. Sun Life is a large insurer of medical stop-loss. Stop-loss is insurance protection for large claims. It is purchased by employers who have self-funded health plans where the employer is assuming the claims risk. Stop-loss provides insurance protection against catastrophic claims. Sun Life insures over 4.7 million people under their stop-loss contracts. The prevalence of claimants with claims of $1 million or more increased 98% between 2014, when the ACA was fully implemented, and 2018, according to Sun Life's data. The likelihood of someone having a claim of $2 million or more increased threefold over the same period. (2) The increased prevalence of catastrophic claims increases insurance volatility and cost. The network contract outlier provisions contribute to these cost problems.

Certain individuals with end-stage renal disease become eligible for Medicare without regard to age because of the high cost of these claims. I am not suggesting we move claimants with claims of $1 million or more to Medicare; that would create patient and provider confusion and would be an administrative nightmare. It would also add unnecessary claim liability, further straining Medicare's financial position. I *am* suggesting that all claims over a specified dollar threshold—let's say $100,000—convert to a Medicare reimbursement schedule or at least a balance-billing limit. This threshold and methodology would apply to both medical and pharmaceutical claims. Reimbursing these high-cost claims at Medicare reimbursement rates would dramatically decrease volatility, lower cost, and increase health insurance competition and could be done administratively behind the scenes with no negative impact to the patient.

A Medicare network access fee could be created to generate Medicare revenue linked to the insurance company and consumer benefit of accessing Medicare reimbursements. This would generate revenue to sustain Medicare without adding to Medicare expenditures and would result in a net decrease in the cost of private health insurance.

Insurance companies could easily handle the changes in reimbursement provisions. The pain point is with the hospitals and pharmaceutical manufacturers. Total hospital profitability would drop with the declining reimbursements from catastrophic claims. Therefore, the hospital industry lobby would voice strong opposition and would likely claim that the link to Medicare reimbursement would decrease care quality and patient access to care. Democrats and Republicans are promising federal government action to lower the impact of rising drug costs on Medicare. The Medicare link for catastrophic claimants would connect the private health insurance system to Medicare reimbursement for these high-cost claimants. I would anticipate strong opposition from the pharmaceutical industry similar to that from the hospital lobby.

It is possible to lower the cost of health insurance and healthcare for everyone. The ACA was really health insurance reform and dramatically regulated the insurance component of healthcare cost. Lowering the cost for everyone means we must reform the actual delivery and cost of healthcare.

Sources

(1)   Center for Responsive Politics. Opensecrets.org.

(2)   Sun Life. "Sun Life Stop-Loss Research Report." Sunlife.com. June 2019.

Chapter 25:

Priority 4—Cover Everyone . . . Finally

IF HEALTHCARE IS A RIGHT, then you lose your right to not have it. We can't have it both ways. Either everyone in America is insured or you maintain your right to choose whether to have health insurance. I am not convinced everyone in America must have health insurance, but I would feel much better if they did. I have never been without health insurance and have never been much of a utilizer of the system. To this point, I have been a combination of lucky and healthy. That said, I would not feel good about my role as a husband and father if my spouse and children lacked the financial and health-access security of health insurance. I know there are millions of dads, moms, husbands, wives, and individuals who find themselves in this uncomfortable position. With a little bit of tough love, compromise, and personal responsibility, I believe universal coverage is within reach . . . for everyone.

CHARACTERISTICS OF THE UNINSURED

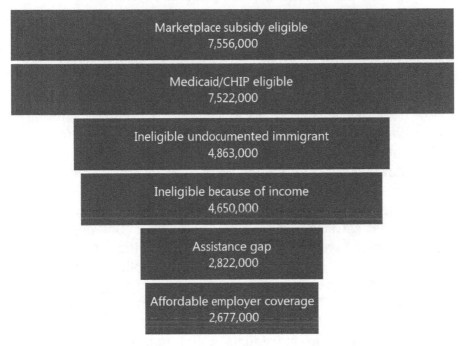

Marketplace subsidy eligible
7,556,000

Medicaid/CHIP eligible
7,522,000

Ineligible undocumented immigrant
4,863,000

Ineligible because of income
4,650,000

Assistance gap
2,822,000

Affordable employer coverage
2,677,000

Source: Linda Blumberg, John Holahan, Michael Karpman, and Caroline Elmendorf. "Characteristics of the Remaining Uninsured: An Update." Urban.org. July 11, 2018.

Trying to tackle the challenge of insuring the uninsured seems impossible if we view the uninsured as a single, homogenous group. Similar to the saying about how to eat an elephant, we will address the uninsured population one bite at a time. Each group gets its own bite.

- **Obamacare Marketplace Subsidy Eligible**—In what might be my most unpopular recommendation in the book (and that list is getting long), the penalty for not having coverage not only needs to be reinstated but it needs to be increased to be equal to the average cost of the annual premium. The Obamacare subsidies cover 86% of the average premium cost. In spite of the substantial financial support, enrollment has not met expectations. For every ten people who enroll in the subsidized Marketplace, almost nine are eligible for a subsidy but have elected to be uninsured. Is it a sign of tough love if medical providers turn away any subsidy-eligible person unwilling to immediately sign up for health insurance? Requiring insurance protects the hospitals, doctors, and taxpayers. Enrollment and eligibility rules in the Marketplace would need to be altered to accommodate this tough-love action.

- **Medicaid/CHIP Eligible**—If I were a health czar, those individuals who are eligible for Medicaid or CHIP would not have a choice to be covered. Our hospitals are required to treat anyone who arrives at the door. The requirement of the hospital to provide care without a responsibility from the patient to enroll in an available organized insurance system that could pay for the care does not make sense and should not be acceptable. It's bad business and bad politics. If a person qualifies for Medicaid or CHIP, any interaction with public services should trigger enrollment. Showing up at a hospital, urgent care facility, or doctor's office should require enrollment. Accessing food stamps, enrolling in school, or any other government interaction should trigger mandatory enrollment. This may sound tough, but sometimes tough love is best. Covering the Medicaid, CHIP, and Marketplace subsidy-eligible individuals would reduce the number of uninsured Americans by over 50%. Two bites consume half the elephant!

- **Not Lawfully Present**—The participants in the second Democratic presidential debate of 2019 were asked to raise their hand if they supported free healthcare for undocumented immigrants. Every hand on the stage went up. I am not showing my hand either way! This is an immigration issue more than a healthcare issue. I am not trying to fix immigration, so on to the next group!

- **Ineligible for Subsidy Because Income Exceeds 400% of the FPL**—This group earns enough to afford health insurance but is choosing to not purchase it. Some in this group are young and healthy and realize the government-manipulated age banding has them subsidizing the cost for older participants. Some simply don't want to comply with anything President Obama implemented. Some make enough money that they are simply willing to accept the risk. This particular group of uninsured individuals is difficult to appease because they can afford health insurance but choose not to buy it. Expanding the subsidies to apply to those who make above 400% of the FPL might help. Offering access to a public-plan option or to Medicare in the individual market might lower the cost of insurance enough to draw them in. A stronger penalty for noncoverage would move many in the group to purchase coverage, but they would probably vote me out of office if I voted to do this to them. Remember, I am trying to solve the problem and not trying to win an election! Unfortunately, I think the combination of more affordable options and a stronger penalty is the only way to close the coverage gap for this final group.

- **Assistance Gap (Ineligible for Subsidy or Medicaid Because of State Non-expansion)**—This one is the most difficult politically to fix because the Supreme Court determined that the federal government can't force states to expand Medicaid eligibility. This has left some of the neediest in society with no financial assistance from either Medicaid or the Marketplace. These individuals earn less than the FPL but are not eligible for assistance through either program. Some of the neediest adults in America do not qualify for any type of health-insurance financial assistance. If you pause to think about this for very long, it is difficult to swallow, regardless of your political beliefs. Some combination of block grants, waivers, or other financing techniques should allow states access to funds to help the neediest in their states. States and the federal government must get together to resolve the Medicaid-expansion stalemate. If not, we should vote all of them out!

- **Ineligible for Subsidy Because of Employer Coverage**—Some individuals and families are stuck between available employer-sponsored coverage and the subsidized Marketplace. Single coverage for the employee is deemed affordable, and this affordability disqualifies all family members for Marketplace assistance. A simple fix is to give eligible individuals the choice between employer-sponsored coverage and coverage through the subsidized Marketplace.

Effective healthcare reform can only happen when rights and responsibilities are inextricably joined. Every right has a corresponding responsibility, and this includes the right to healthcare. The personal and social responsibilities include:

- the responsibility to dramatically improve cost efficiency and care-quality outcomes of the American healthcare system for all Americans;

- the responsibility to provide a public health insurance safety net for the neediest in our communities;

- the responsibility to provide financial support for those who cannot afford to pay health insurance premiums on their own;

- the responsibility to offer the financial protection of health insurance coverage for the employees and families of our companies; and

- the responsibility to adequately fund today's public health insurance programs so that tomorrow's taxpayers don't have to fund today's expenses.

Maybe "Healthcare Is a Responsibility!" should be a campaign sign!

Section Closing

The perceived degree of change needed in healthcare is linked to your perception of the problem. How severe are the patient's (the healthcare system's) symptoms? Are they a mere inconvenience, or are they life-threatening? A person with a wart on their finger might want the wart removed. Amputating the person's arm or performing major surgery on the finger, followed by chemotherapy and radiation, would get rid of the wart; however, the side effects of the treatments would not be worth the inconvenience of the problem. The treatment must be appropriate for the problem. Does our healthcare system need some diet and exercise, physical therapy, minimally invasive surgery, major reconstructive surgery, or a complete transplant? The politicians are stating their case for their prescribed course of treatment. They range from *take two aspirin and call me in four years* to a complete organ transplant of the entire healthcare system.

I believe the healthcare problems for our country's economic future and the problems for both insured and uninsured families are real. I also believe now is the time to take corrective action. Ignoring the symptoms will only make the condition worse. The risks and rewards of the total-transplant approach feels out of balance to me, but it might work for you, and it might work for enough voters to make it a reality. I believe sustaining Medicare, reducing cost for everyone, protecting access, and covering everyone is achievable and appropriate. Some might consider my recommended course of treatment as incremental and minimally invasive because it leaves all current stakeholders in place with adjusted and aligned roles. Some might consider my recommended course of action as too aggressive, major surgery with considerable pain, risk, and rehabilitation. My hope is that this book increases your understanding of our current system; provides insight into the painful symptoms of our current healthcare system and their root causes; equips you to listen critically to the presidential candidates' proposals; and, most importantly, allows you as a voter to form *your* opinion of how to best reform healthcare in America.

9 781457 570711